QUILTING
In No Time

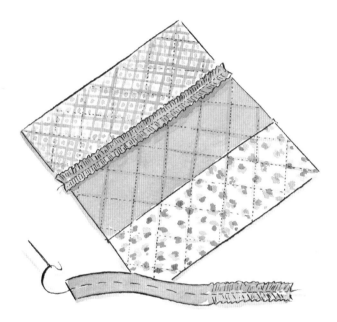

QUILTING
In No Time

50 step-by-step weekend projects made easy

Emma Hardy

CICO BOOKS
LONDON NEW YORK

Published in 2009 by CICO Books
an imprint of Ryland Peters & Small
519 Broadway, 5th Floor, New York, NY 10012

www.cicobooks.co.uk

10 9 8 7 6 5 4 3 2 1

A CIP catalog record for this book is available from the Library of Congress.

Paperback ISBN-13: 978 1 906525 30 9
Hardcover ISBN-13: 978 1 60751 523 4

Printed in China

Editor: Marie Clayton
Designer: Liz Sephton
Photographer: Debbie Patterson
Illustrator: Michael Hill

Contents

Introduction

Patchwork and quilting have long been used as a way of creating home furnishings and clothing from scraps of fabric. In the 1800s European immigrants took their skills to America, where they were embraced by the early settlers, as an economical way of producing items from old materials. The craft, however, can be traced back much further than this with the earliest examples dating back several thousand years.

In more recent times, quilting and patchwork have become an art form as well as a practical craft and there has been a huge resurgence in the last 50 years. Often thought of as slightly old-fashioned the craft has been taken up by younger, more design-aware crafters who are taking the traditions of quilting and using them in a more contemporary way.

With such an extensive range of fabrics available to us, we no longer have to "make do" with leftover scraps of fabric, and projects can be designed with specific fabrics in mind incorporating beautiful patterns and colors with stunning results. However, making something from scraps, using leftover pieces of favorite fabrics and eking out small pieces of expensive cloth to create something beautiful is a deeply satisfying process and in our environmentally aware times, can be a great way to recycle and reuse.

In this book I have put together 50 projects ranging from simple coasters that can be made in less than an hour to larger pillows and quilts that take slightly longer to make but none requiring more than a couple of days to complete. With the emphasis on simplicity and style, the projects are designed to be suitable for the novice stitcher as well as the long-time crafter and will fit into all areas of your home, with lots of ideas that would make great gifts, too. Beautifully illustrated, easy-to-follow, step-by-step instructions will lead you confidently through each project and a handy techniques section explains some basic skills with tips on cutting out, piecing, and stitching. The projects in this book are all relatively quick to make and include a guide to the amount of time required to complete each one, presuming that you have some sewing experience. Add a little extra time if you are new to needlework.

One of the wonderful things about patchwork and quilting is that there are no limits to the number of original and beautiful results possible. With this in mind, I hope you will be inspired to create many wonderful patchwork projects of your own using and adapting the ideas in this book.

CHAPTER 1

Relaxation Spaces

Sofa Throw

Created from staggered rectangles of fabrics in shades of green and brown, this stylish sofa throw is surprisingly easy to make. As with many quilts, it takes longer to cut out the patchwork pieces than it takes to stitch them together. Speed up the process by using a rotary cutter (see the techniques section) so that several layers of fabric can be cut at the same time. This quilt is backed with fine linen, which drapes beautifully and is hard wearing.

MATERIALS

Enough fabric to make 64 rectangles measuring 6 x 8in
79in by the full fabric width of plain natural linen
67 x 51in of cotton batting
5 buttons

6 hours

1. Cut a paper pattern rectangle measuring 6 x 8in. Use this to cut out 64 fabric rectangles in various fabrics. Lay them on the work surface in a row of eight lengthwise and with right sides together, pin and stitch them together along the short sides, using a ⅞in seam. Press the seams open. Repeat using the remaining fabric rectangles to create eight strips of eight rectangles.

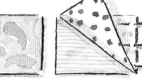

2. With right sides together, pin and stitch these strips together, staggering the seams so that each vertical seam of a new strip falls exactly in the middle of a rectangle on the previous strip. Continue in this way to join all the strips together. Press the seams open and trim the protruding ends of the strips to form a neat panel of patchwork that measures 41⅞ x 53⅞in.

3. Measure and cut two strips of linen 42 x 2¾in. With right sides together, pin and stitch one strip along one end of the patchwork panel (the end being the side with the shorter widths of rectangles). Repeat at the other end with the second strip of linen. Cut two more strips of linen 61 x 2¾in. With right sides together, pin and stitch along both sides of the patchwork and press the seams open.

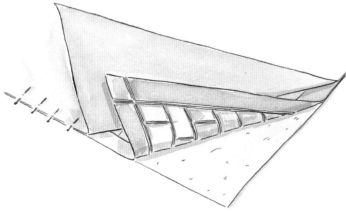

4. Measure and cut a piece of batting and a piece of linen 61 x 47in. Lay the patchwork panel wrong side down onto the batting, smoothing out the layers to make sure that they are completely flat. Lay the linen fabric over the patchwork and pin and stitch through all the layers all the way round, leaving an opening of about 12in along one edge. Snip the corners and turn the throw the right way out. Hand stitch the opening and press the whole throw. Sew buttons randomly onto the throw, stitching through all layers to join them.

Log Cabin Pillow Cover

This is a very traditional patchwork, which takes its name from the log cabins built by the early American pioneers. The central panel was traditionally red, representing the hearth, with the surrounding strips, which are all slightly longer than the preceding one, forming the logs around it. I have used a selection of red fabrics here, which all complement each other nicely. Experiment with fabrics in lighter and darker tones for a different effect.

MATERIALS
Scraps of fabric 4in wide by the width of the fabric
19¾ x 32in piece of fabric for the back of the cover
18in square pillow form

←2 hours→

1. Measure and cut a 2¾in square of one of the fabrics. Make strips of your fabrics 2½in wide by the width of the fabric. The best way to do this is to make a small snip at the edge of the fabric 2½in from the edge and tear from the snip. Press all the strips. Cut a piece of one of the strips 2¾in long and with right sides together, pin and stitch it to one side of the fabric square. Press the seam open.

2. Take a strip of a different fabric and cut a length, which should be the width of the center square plus the width of the first strip. With right sides together, pin and stitch this strip in place. Press the seam open.

3. Using a strip of fabric in another design, cut a strip for the next side as before and pin and stitch it to the main patchwork panel with right sides together. Press the seam open.

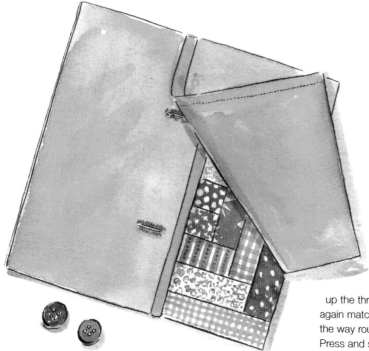

4. Cut another strip for the fourth side, which will be the width of the center square plus two widths of fabric strips. Stitch in place as before and press.

5. Continue to build up the patchwork adding strips around it, making sure that you work in a clockwise direction without missing out any sides. Increase the length of the strips to fit each side until the panel measures 19in square. Press.

6. For the back of the cover, measure and cut two rectangles of fabric 19 x 16in. Fold under ¼in along one long side of each and press. Fold over another ¾in and pin and stitch in place. On one of the pieces work two buttonholes (follow the directions in your sewing machine manual to make these). Lay this rectangle with right sides together onto the patchwork, matching up the three raw edges. Lay the second rectangle onto this, again matching up the raw edges. Pin and machine stitch all the way round. Snip the corners and turn the right way out. Press and stitch buttons onto the back, lining them up with the buttonholes. Fill the pillow cover with the pillow form.

Three Panel Patch Pillow

This patchwork is called rail fence and is made up of blocks of three bars of fabric, which are joined in a nine-patch block. I have used fabrics of a similar color and tone for a random patchwork, but it can be made with three different colored fabrics, which can form an attractive zigzag pattern. As with lots of the projects that are made from square blocks joined together, just add more blocks to form a larger patchwork panel to fit a larger pillow—or even make into a quilt.

1. Draw and cut a rectangle of paper 8 x 3in to make a paper pattern. Using the paper pattern cut out nine rectangles of each of the three fabrics, so you have 27 in total. With right sides together, pin and stitch one rectangle of each fabric together along the longest sides. Vary the order of the fabrics so that the overall patchwork will be random.

2 hours

MATERIALS

10 x 36in of each of three different fabrics for the patchwork
Paper for the pattern
24 x 32in piece of fabric for the backing
22in square pillow form

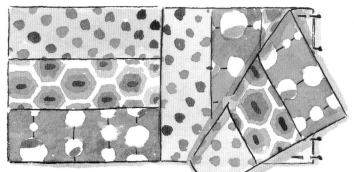

2. Press the seams open and continue to create nine patchwork squares, each made of three rectangles. With right sides together, pin and stitch three of the squares together to form a strip. Arrange them with the bars horizontally, then vertically and the third square horizontally again. Repeat this with the next three squares, laying the bars vertically this time and then horizontally and the last square vertically. Use the last three squares to create a strip like the first one. Press the seams open.

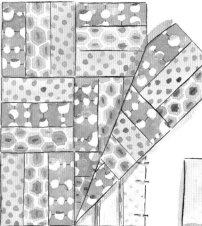

3. With right sides together, pin and stitch the three strips together in their correct order to create the front of the pillow cover. Press the seams open.

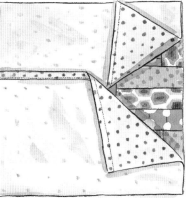

4. To make the back of the pillow cover, cut two rectangles of fabric measuring 23 x 16in. Fold over ½in along one long side of each piece and again by another 1¼in. Pin and stitch close to the first fold on both pieces. Lay the patchwork panel right side up on the work surface and lay one of the back pieces onto it with right sides together, lining up the raw edges. Place the second back piece onto the patchwork panel, again lining up the raw edges, so that the hemmed edges overlap each other. Pin and stitch all the way round. Snip the corners off and turn the right way out. Press. Fill the pillow cover with the pillow form.

Bolster

A bolster adds an interesting decorative touch to a sofa, as well as adding an extra degree of comfort. This bolster cover is made by joining strips of fabric to form a panel, which is then stitched to cover the pillow. This design means that there is no need to sew a zipper or buttons and buttonholes onto the cover, because the simple drawstring ends make it simple to fill it with the pillow form and remove it to clean.

1½ hours

MATERIALS

18 x 7in bolster pillow

18 x 24in piece of main fabric

4 x 24in each of three more coordinating fabrics

Fabric for piping

48in length of piping cord

44in length of ribbon

1. Measure and cut a piece of main fabric 11½ x 22in. Cut two strips of one of the coordinating fabrics each 2¼ x 22in. With right sides together, pin and stitch a strip onto either side of the main piece of fabric. Press the seams open.

2. Measure and cut two strips of a second coordinating fabric 1¾ x 22in. With right sides together, pin and stitch a strip onto either side of the main panel, pressing the seams open again.

3. Cut another two strips from the third coordinating fabric measuring 1¾ x 22in. Again, with right sides together, pin and stitch a strip onto either side of the main panel and press the seams open.

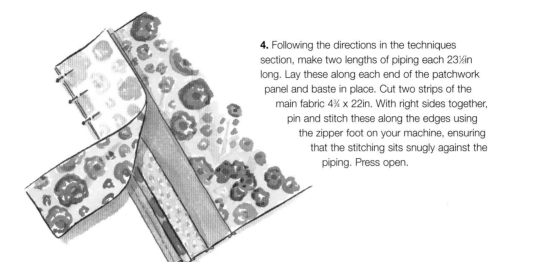

4. Following the directions in the techniques section, make two lengths of piping each 23½in long. Lay these along each end of the patchwork panel and baste in place. Cut two strips of the main fabric 4¾ x 22in. With right sides together, pin and stitch these along the edges using the zipper foot on your machine, ensuring that the stitching sits snugly against the piping. Press open.

5. Fold the patchwork panel in half with right sides together and pin and stitch along the longest side.

6. Fold under ½in to the wrong side at each end of the tube and press. Fold over by another ½in and pin and slip stitch in place, leaving a gap of about ⅝in in the stitching.

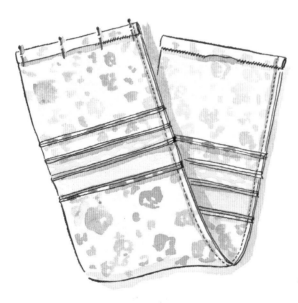

7. Cut two lengths of ribbon about 22in long. Attach a safety pin through one end of one of the ribbons and push it through the channel at the end of the fabric tube until it comes back out through the hole. Remove the safety pin and pull the ribbon to gather the fabric, finishing with a bow. Push the bolster into the cover and thread the ribbon through the other end, again finishing with a bow.

Curtain

This traditional patchwork design is made up of sets of eight triangles pieced together to form squares, which are then joined together to make a larger panel. To hang the patchwork up at a window, attach curtain clips at regular intervals across the top and thread onto a curtain rod. A curtain like this can be made to fit any size of window by simply adding more patchwork squares to the length and width. Using a lightweight batting to line the curtain means that it will drape nicely, but will still help prevent drafts and keep your home cozy during colder weather.

MATERIALS

20 x 49in pieces of each of eight different fabrics
43½in square of fabric for backing
43½in square of light-weight batting
12 buttons
Needle and thread

4 hours

The finished curtain is 42⅞in square. For a larger curtain, make more patchwork squares and add to the width or length as needed.

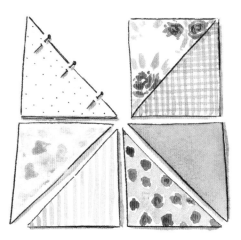

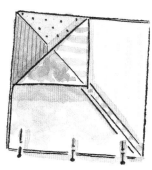

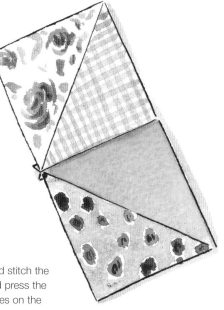

1. Using the template on page 169, cut a paper triangle for your pattern. Use this to cut nine triangles of each of the eight fabrics. Take one triangle of each fabric and lay on the work surface to form a square. With right sides together, pin and stitch the two triangles at the top left together and press the seam open. Trim the seam allowance at the corners. Repeat this with the other triangles in the square to form four small squares.

2. With right sides together, pin and stitch the two left hand squares together and press the seam open. Repeat with the squares on the right hand side.

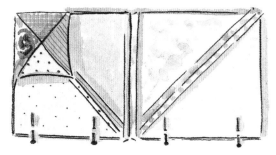

3. Take the two strips and stitch them together with right sides together to make a square. Match up the seams neatly. Press the seam open. Repeat these steps with the remaining fabric triangles to make eight more squares, keeping the position of each fabric in each square the same.

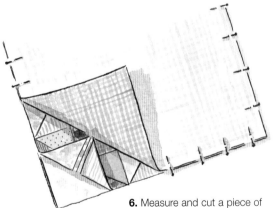

4. Take three of the squares and with right sides together, pin and stitch them together, keeping all the squares the same way up. Press the seams open. Join the remaining squares to make three strips of three squares.

5. To make the curtain, join these three strips together by stitching them with right sides together to make a large square panel. Press the seams open. Press the front of the panel.

6. Measure and cut a piece of batting and a piece of backing fabric 42⅛in square. Lay the patchwork panel right side up onto the batting and position the backing fabric on top of this. Ensure that all the layers are completely flat and pin and stitch all the way round, leaving an opening of about 12in along one side. Snip the corners off and turn the right way out and hand stitch the opening closed. Press. Sew buttons onto the curtain to join all the layers together at the join of the triangles.

Pouffe

There is something very satisfying about creating a piece of furniture from scraps of fabric! This pouffe is made from a nine-patch panel on the top with panels of six squares along each side; a solid square of fabric is then stitched onto the bottom (although you could make another nine-patch panel following the steps for the top). When filled with stuffing, the pouffe forms a solid shape. Try recycling old blankets or woolen clothes for a more vintage look, or use squares of corduroy in different colors to striking effect.

MATERIALS

24in squares of each of four wool fabrics
20in square of fabric for the base
Paper for pattern
39 x 53in of stiff iron-on interfacing
Stuffing

⟵2 hours⟶

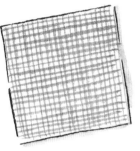

1. Draw a 6¾in square onto paper and cut out to use as your pattern to cut 33 squares of fabric (eight each of three fabrics and nine of one). Take nine of the squares and arrange them in three rows of three, making sure that no two squares of the same fabric are next to each other. With right sides together, pin and stitch three of the squares together to form a strip.

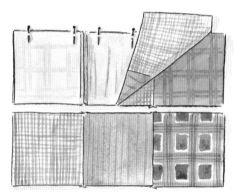

2. Repeat this with the remaining six squares to form three strips of three squares. Press the seams open. With right sides together, pin and stitch these strips together to form a square. Press the seams open. Following the manufacturer's directions, iron stiff interfacing to the back of this panel.

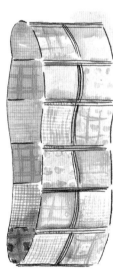

3. Join more squares together in this way to make four panels of six squares. Following the manufacturer's directions, iron stiff interfacing to the wrong side of each panel. With right sides together, join these panels together to form a long strip two squares wide and 12 squares long. Join the ends together to form a loop.

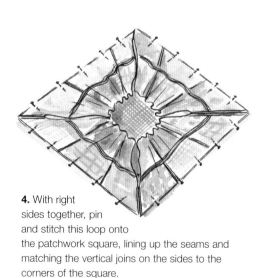

4. With right sides together, pin and stitch this loop onto the patchwork square, lining up the seams and matching the vertical joins on the sides to the corners of the square.

5. Measure and cut a 19¼in square of one of the fabrics and iron interfacing to the wrong side. With right sides together, pin and stitch this to the rest of the pouffe, leaving an opening of about 8in along one side. Snip all the corners and turn the right way out. Press.

6. Stuff the pouffe, pushing the stuffing into all the corners to form a neat cube. Pack the stuffing firmly in for a more solid pouffe, or use slightly less for a saggier look. Hand stitch the opening closed.

Rug

Strip patchwork has been used to make this striking rug that mixes bold bright patterns with a small-scale gingham to create some definition. Strips of fabric in different widths create a random-looking patchwork, which has been lined with a medium weight batting and backed with a heavy-weight cotton to help it withstand wear and tear.

MATERIALS

Selection of different fabrics each at least 40in long

Plain white cotton fabric at least 40in long by the width of the finished rug

Heavy-weight cotton batting at least 40in long by the width of the finished rug

Fabric for the backing at least 48in long and 8in wider than the finished rug

1. Measure and cut strips of fabric in varying widths all 40in long and at least 4in wide. Lay them onto the work surface in a pleasing arrangement. With right sides together, pin and stitch the strips together, pressing the seams open as you work. The finished panel should be about 20in wide. Add more strips if you would like a wider rug.

2. Cut a piece of batting and a piece of white cotton fabric to the same size as the patchwork panel. Lay the cotton onto the work surface with the batting on the top and the patchwork on top of that. Pin all the layers together to hold them in place. Machine stitch along the seams to quilt the layers together.

3. For the backing, cut a piece of fabric measuring 48in long and 4in wider on each side than the patchwork panel. Press under ½in all the way round it. Lay it on the work surface wrong side up and place the quilted patchwork panel centrally onto it, right side up. Turn over the backing fabric overlapping the raw edge of the patchwork by ½in and pin in place to create the border. Machine stitch in place and repeat along the opposite side.

4. Repeat step 3 along the two remaining ends of the rug, pinning the border in place and machine stitching to finish. Press.

Draft Excluder

Keep the drafts at bay with this sweet draft excluder. Strips of fabric are joined together to form a long sausage shape, which is then filled with stuffing to help keep your home cozy and warm. Try to buy cotton stuffing rather than synthetic, as it is much weightier. If this is unavailable, put some dried beans or rice inside with the stuffing to make it heavier.

MATERIALS
Scraps of fabric at least 15in long
45in length of bobble fringe
45in of ribbon
Stuffing

1½ hours

1. Cut strips of fabric in varying widths each 15in long. Move them around until you are happy with the arrangement. With right sides together and starting at one end, pin and stitch two of the strips together. Press the seam open.

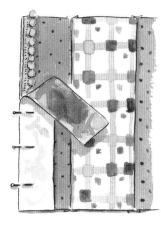

2. Continue to join the strips in this way, pressing the seams open as you go. To add the bobble fringe, lay a length of it along one raw edge of fabric (right side) and baste in position. Lay the next strip into this with right sides together and machine stitch. The finished panel should be about 34in long (although you may wish to make a longer version for a wider door). Add more strips if you are making a longer one.

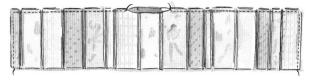

3. Pin and stitch lengths of ribbon randomly along the seams, trimming the ends to neaten them. Fold the fabric over with right sides together, pin and stitch along all three sides (not the folded side), leaving an opening of about 6in. Trim the corners and turn the right way out. Press.

4. Fill the cover with stuffing, pushing it into the corners and spreading it evenly inside. Hand stitch the opening closed.

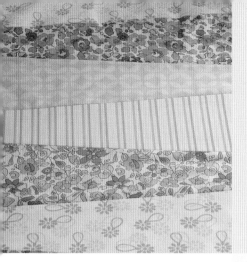

CHAPTER 2

Kitchens & Dining Rooms

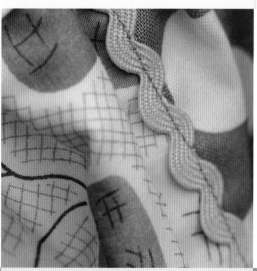

Triangle Patchwork Tablecloth

This tablecloth constructed from triangles of alternate red and off-white fabrics adds a crisp, fresh touch to a dining table. Patches of a selection of red fabrics are placed next to patches of plain fabric to unify the pattern and highlight the patchwork design. I have backed the cloth in linen, which adds a lovely weight and helps the cloth to drape beautifully. As with many of the projects in this book, the use can easily be changed—this would also make a beautiful quilt or throw.

MATERIALS

Selection of bold stripes, ginghams, and patterned fabric in one basic color
51 x 36in piece of polka dot fabric with a pale background
47 x 63in piece of striped fabric for the backing
Paper for pattern
14 buttons

6 hours

1. Using the template on page 172, cut a paper pattern triangle. Use this to cut out 56 triangles using a selection of your basic color fabrics and a further 48 triangles in the polka dot fabric. Cut the triangle pattern in half and cut 16 half triangles from the polka dot fabric. With right sides together, pin and stitch a colored triangle onto a polka dot half triangle, pressing the seam to the polka dot triangle side. Continue using alternate triangles until you have a strip six polka dot triangles long with a half triangle at each end.

2. Trim the ends of the seams to make neat rows. When you have eight rows, with right sides together, pin and stitch them together. Press the seams open at the back. Press the whole cloth.

3. Cut a piece of backing fabric 45 x 59½in. With right sides together, pin and stitch this to the patchwork cloth, leaving an opening of about 8in along one side. Snip the corners, turn the cloth the right way out, and hand stitch the opening closed.

4. Sew buttons onto the outer alternate triangles, stitching through both layers, and then press.

Napkin

Beautiful fabric napkins can add the finishing touch to your dining and this napkin design is so easy to make that a whole set can be created in no time at all. They are a simplified version of the traditional log cabin design, made by adding strips of fabric around a central square. A bold patterned fabric forms the border, complemented by a strong plain color in the middle, with a more delicate pattern sandwiched between them that is used as the backing as well.

1 hour

MATERIALS

10in piece of 45in wide plain fabric

63in piece of 45in wide patterned fabric A

30in piece of 45in wide patterned fabric B

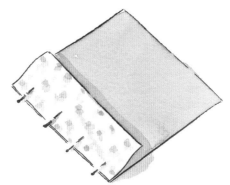

1. Measure and cut out a piece of plain fabric 7½in square. Cut a strip of patterned fabric A measuring 2½in wide by the width of the fabric. Cut a length of this 7½in long and with right sides together, pin and stitch it to one side of the plain fabric square with a ¼in seam. Press the seam open.

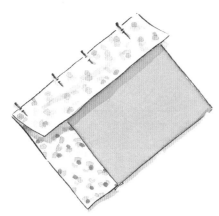

2. Cut another length from the strip of patterned fabric 9½in long and with right sides together, pin and stitch it to the next side of the panel. Press the seam open. Cut another strip of patterned fabric 9½in long and stitch along the third side of the panel, then press the seam open. Finish with a fourth strip measuring 11½in sewn onto the last side of the panel. Press the seam open.

3. Cut strips of patterned fabric B again 2½in wide from the width of the fabric. Cut a length 11½in long and pin and stitch to one side of the patchwork panel with right sides together. Press the seam open. Cut another length of fabric 13½in long and stitch onto the next side, with a third piece 13½in long and a fourth piece 15½in long to complete the patchwork.

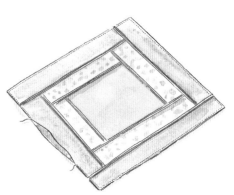

4. Cut a piece of patterned fabric A measuring 15½in square and with right sides together, pin and stitch the patchwork panel to this, leaving an opening of about 2in along one side. Snip the corners and turn the right way out. Hand stitch the opening closed and press. Repeat steps 1 to 4 to make another five napkins.

Napkin Rings

These lovely napkin rings are the perfect project for using up scraps of fabric that would otherwise be discarded. Thin strips of fabric are joined together to make a panel, which is then cut into pieces, creating a whole set that would make a unique and much treasured wedding or anniversary gift. To use up even smaller scraps of fabric, make each band separately using shorter lengths for a more individual and casual effect.

1½ hours

MATERIALS

Scraps of coordinating fabric

100in rickrack braid

12 x 8in piece of cotton batting

4 buttons

1. To make four napkin rings measure and cut 12 strips of fabric 1½ x 10in. Lay them on the work surface side by side and move them around until you are happy with the arrangement. With right sides together, pin and stitch the strips together with a ¼in seam, pressing the seams open as you work.

2. Cut the panel in half and then into half again so that you have four equal size striped strips. Cut four pieces of fabric 12½ x 2½in. Lay a patchwork piece right side up on the work surface and lay a length of rickrack along each edge with the edge of the rickrack lined up with the raw edge of the panel. Baste in position. Lay a strip of fabric on top of this with right sides together. Machine stitch along both sides from the edge. Turn the right way out. Repeat on the other three sets of strips.

3. Turn one raw end in by ½in and hand stitch closed. Cut a piece of batting 12 x 2in and push inside the tube of fabric, making sure that it lies flat and is pushed right into the corners. Turn the remaining raw end in by ½in and hand stitch closed.

4. Overlap the ends of the strip by 1in to form a ring and hand stitch in place, finishing with a button sewn on. Repeat steps 3 and 4 for the other three napkin rings.

Place Mat

2 hours

This cute flower place mat brings an element of fun to a table setting. Fabric cut into petal shapes is pieced together and finished with a central circle edged in rickrack. The mat has been lined with interfacing to make it slightly thicker, so protecting the tabletop from hot dishes and creating a more starched finish to the mat.

MATERIALS

Scraps of fabric each at least
14½ x 5½in

14in square of fabric for backing

Paper for pattern

14in square of iron-on interfacing

18in length of rickrack

1. Using the template on page 170, cut a pattern piece. Use this to cut 12 petal shapes from four different fabrics. Arrange them so that no two petals of the same color are next to each other. With right sides together, pin and stitch three petals together and press the seams open. Repeat with the other petals.

2. With right sides together, pin and stitch two of the three-petal patches together to form a semicircle of petals. Press the seams open. Repeat to make a second semicircle.

3. Lay one of the petal semicircles onto the other one with right sides together. Pin and stitch them together and press the seams open. Press the whole patchwork on the right side.

4. Lay the patchwork flower onto the backing fabric, pin and use as a pattern to cut out the flower shape. Cut a piece of interfacing to fit this backing piece and, following the manufacturer's directions, iron it onto the wrong side of the backing fabric. Lay the patchwork onto the backing fabric with right sides together, and pin and stitch all the way round but leaving a gap of about 1¼in. Make small snips in the seam allowance all round the flower. Turn the right way out through the gap and press.

5 Cut out two circles of fabric with a diameter of 4¾in. Pin with right sides together and stitch round them leaving an opening of about 1¼in. Make small snips all round the seam allowance and turn the right way out. Hand stitch the opening closed and press.

6. Place the circle exactly centrally in the patchwork flower. Pin and machine stitch in place. Take the rickrack and pin it around the circle. Machine stitch in place, overlapping the ends neatly. Press the place mat.

Table Runner

A table runner can protect your dining table as well as adding a decorative touch. This quilted version is the perfect place to put hot dishes and bowls when serving up a meal. It is made from irregular rectangles pieced together by topping and tailing them to create a long strip. Make yours long enough to fit from one end of the table to the other, with enough to hang down slightly at either end. Hand quilting can be a rather slow process but is perfect for a project of this size and holds the layers together beautifully.

MATERIALS
24 x 16in approx of fabric in five different designs
16 x 59in cotton batting
16 x 59in piece of fabric for the backing
Embroidery thread and needle
Paper for pattern

3 hours

1. Using the template on page 172, cut out a paper pattern. Pin this to the fabrics that you are using and cut out four pieces in each fabric (20 pieces in total). Arrange the pieces, topping and tailing them and ensuring that no two pieces of the same fabric are next to each other. With right sides together, pin and stitch the pieces together, pressing the seams open as you go. Continue until all 20 pieces are joined together.

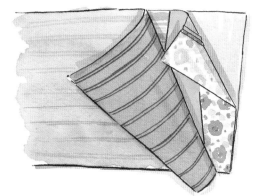

2. Lay the patchwork strip onto the batting, smoothing it out to remove any folds and creases, and cut out the shape. Repeat this using the backing fabric, making sure that the patchwork and the backing fabric are wrong sides together when you cut them out. Lay the patchwork right side up onto the batting and then place the backing fabric right side down (if applicable) onto this. Pin and stitch all the way round, leaving an opening of about 8in along one side.

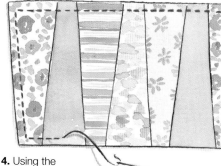

3. Snip the corners of the seams and turn the right way out. Hand stitch the opening closed and press.

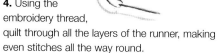

4. Using the embroidery thread, quilt through all the layers of the runner, making even stitches all the way round.

Coasters

Protect your tabletop with these cute coasters, which are the perfect project to get you into quilting. Squares of fabric are joined to make one large square, which is then backed and machine quilted. What could be easier? Use a lighter weight batting so that the coasters lie flat.

1 hour

MATERIALS

18 x 12in piece of fabric in each of two different designs
10 x 10in piece of fabric in a coordinating design
10 x 10in piece of batting

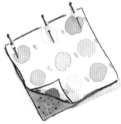

1. Draw a square on paper measuring 3in on each side and cut out to use as a pattern. Using the pattern, cut out two squares each of two different fabrics. With right sides together, pin and stitch two of the squares (one of each fabric) together with a ⅛in seam. Press the seams open.

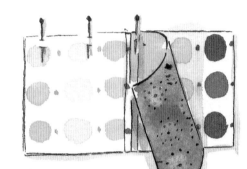

2. With right sides together, pin and stitch the two strips together with a ⅛in seam, ensuring that squares of different fabrics are next to each other in a checkerboard design. Again, press the seam open.

3. Cut a square of the third fabric measuring 5in square and cut a piece of batting to this size. Lay the backing square right side up on the work surface with the patchwork square right side down on top of it. Place the batting square on top of this. Pin and stitch through all layers all the way round, leaving an opening of about ⅛in along one side.

4. Snip the corners and turn the right way out. Hand stitch the opening closed and press. Measure ⅛in in from the edge of the coaster and mark with pins. Top stitch along this line. Measure and mark at equal intervals from this line and top stitch in the same way to quilt the coaster. Repeat steps 1 to 4 to make five more coasters.

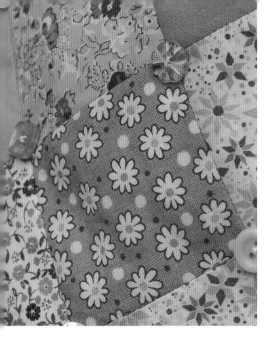

Tea Cozy

Tea cozies need to be well insulated to keep the tea piping hot, and this pretty patchwork cozy fits the bill perfectly. The design creates a great way of using up even the smallest scraps of fabric, and works well using small-scale patterns. Create a dynamic, contemporary look by using small squares of bold prints, or solid colors in different shades. Raid your button box for a selection of pretty buttons to quilt all the layers together and add extra decoration.

MATERIALS

Scraps of fabric to cut 30 2¾in squares
15 x 11in piece of fabric for the backing
15 x 22in piece of fabric for the lining
27in length of bobble fringe
15 x 22in piece of cotton batting
Paper for pattern
12 buttons (approx.)

3 hours

1. With right sides together, pin and stitch the squares together, making sure that no two squares of the same fabric are next to each other. Make three strips of six squares, one strip of five squares, one strip of four squares, and one strip of three squares. Press all the seams open.

2. Following the diagram, and with right sides together, pin and stitch the strips together, starting with the three longer strips, graduating to the shortest strip on the right hand side. Press the seams open.

3. Using the template on page 173, cut a pattern piece and lay it onto the patchwork panel centrally. Pin in place and cut out.

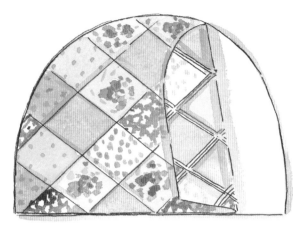

4. Using the paper pattern cut two pieces of batting and a piece of backing fabric.

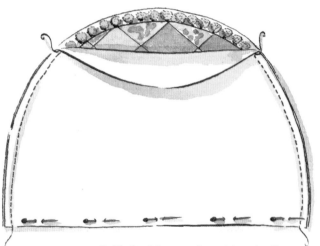

5. Lay the patchwork panel right side up on top of one of the pieces of batting. Lay the bobble fringe all the way round the edge pointing inwards and baste in place. Lay the backing fabric right side down onto this with the other piece of batting on top. Pin and machine stitch all the way round the curve, using the zipper foot on the machine.

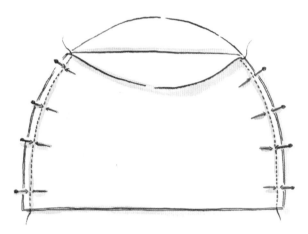

6. Using the paper pattern, cut two lining fabric pieces. With right sides together, pin and stitch them together around the curved edge only, leaving an opening of about 4in at the top.

7. Slip the lining over the patchwork with right sides together, lining up the seams. Pin and stitch around the base.

8. Pull the lining to its right side and hand stitch the opening closed. Push inside the tea cozy. Hand stitch buttons onto the front of the tea cozy, stitching through all the layers to hold them in place.

Apron

Sure to have you reaching for your baking tools, this cute apron is made from strip patchwork and has a real vintage feel. Strips of two different fabrics of equal width are alternated to form the "skirt" and embellished with rickrack in a complementary color. Add a patchwork pocket to make it practical as well as pretty, if you like.

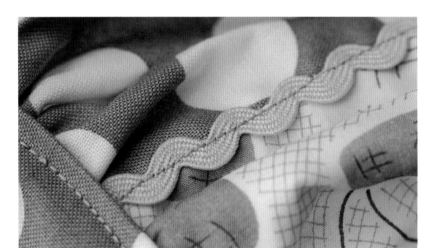

1½ hours

MATERIALS

8in of 54in wide patterned fabric
12in of 54in wide spotted fabric
30in of 54in wide gingham fabric
99in rickrack braid

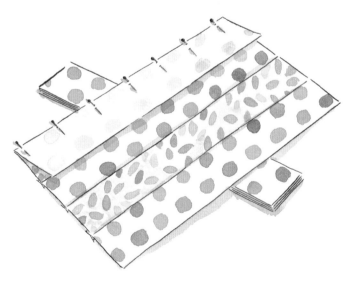

1. To make the apron, measure and cut strips of the patterned and spotted fabrics 3¾in wide by 21½in long. You will need five strips of spotted fabric and four strips of patterned fabric. With right sides together, pin and stitch the strips together, alternating the fabrics but starting and ending with the spotted fabric. Press the seams open.

2. Cut lengths of rickrack 22in long and pin, then stitch them along one side of each of the patterned strips. Trim the ends neatly.

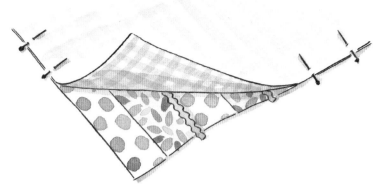

3. Cut a piece of gingham fabric 25¾ x 21½in. With right sides together, pin, then stitch this to the patchwork piece, leaving an opening about 4in long. Snip the corners and turn the right way out through the opening. Press.

4. Make a running stitch across the top of the apron skirt and gather the fabric up to a width of about 18in. Finish with a few stitches to secure the gathering.

5. To make the waistband, measure and cut a strip of spotted fabric and a strip of gingham fabric 2½ x 54in. You can join lengths together if the fabric width is narrower than 54in. With right sides together, pin and stitch the strips together along both ends and one long side. Turn the right way out.

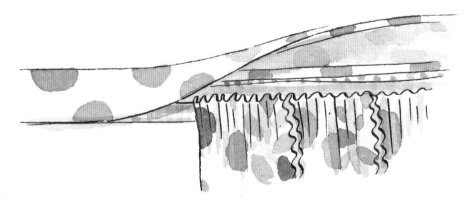

6. Press under ½in along the raw edges of both strips of fabric. Lay the gathered edge of the apron skirt inside the centre of the waistband, placing it up from the edge by ½in, and pin in place. Top stitch along the fold to hold the apron in place, continuing round all edges of the waistband. Press.

Kitchen Curtain

This lightweight patchwork curtain is quick to make and will transform a kitchen or utility room. Large squares of pretty floral fabrics have been teamed with crisp ticking and a plain fabric to break up the pattern. A length of curtain wire threaded through a channel across the top means it is simple to hang in place and take down to launder.

1 hour

MATERIALS

Assorted fabrics to cut into 12in squares
Paper for pattern
Curtain wire and eyelets
2 hooks

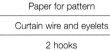

1. Measure and cut out a 12in square of paper. Pin onto the fabrics and cut out squares. Arrange the squares so that no two squares of the same fabric are next to each other, using enough squares to create a panel of the size that you need for your curtain. With right sides together, pin and stitch the squares together working in horizontal lines.

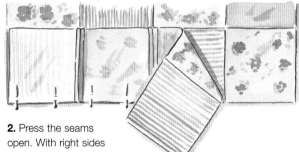

2. Press the seams open. With right sides together, pin and stitch the strips together in the correct order and again press the seams open.

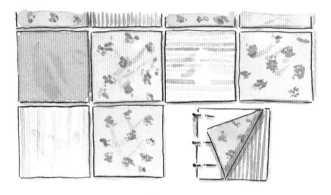

3. Fold over ⅛in along both vertical sides and fold this over again by ¾in. Pin and stitch in place.

4. Fold the top edge and bottom edge over to the wrong side by ⅛in and again by 1¼in. Stitch. Press the curtain. Thread curtain wire with an eyelet at each end through the top channel, then hang in place by attaching the eyelets to the hooks on either side of the window.

Trivet

Make a bright and cheerful trivet to protect your kitchen surfaces. A patchwork square is made from four triangles of fabric that, when lined with thick batting and backed, can be quilted in a sweet flower shape for extra decoration. Choose heavier weight fabric for this project so that it will withstand heat from pans and dishes, but ensure that the fabrics are machine washable.

(1 hour)

MATERIALS

Piece of floral fabric

Scraps of polka dot fabric

9in square of cotton batting

9in square of plain white cotton

Paper for template

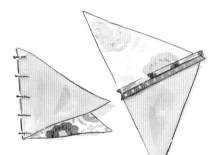

1. Using the template on page 173, cut out two triangles of floral fabric and two of polka dot fabric. With right sides together, pin and stitch a floral triangle to a polka dot triangle. Repeat with the remaining two triangles ensuring that the floral triangle is on the same side in each pair of triangles. Press the seams open.

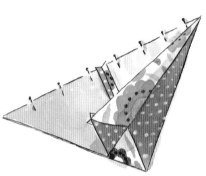

2. With right sides together, pin and stitch the sets of triangles together. Press the seam open.

3. Cut a piece of plain white cotton and a piece of cotton batting both measuring 9in square. Lay the white cotton on the work surface and place the square of batting on top of this. Put the patchwork square right side up on top of the batting. Using the template on page 173, cut out a flower shape. Lay it centrally onto the patchwork panel and pin in place through all layers. Machine stitch around the edge of the flower.

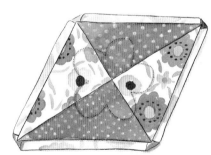

4. Measure and cut a square of floral fabric 10½in square. Place it right side down onto the work surface with the quilted patchwork panel centrally on top of it. Fold the corner over by 1¼in and tuck the corner underneath the quilted panel.

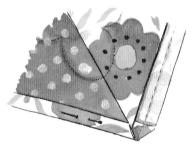

5. Fold the edge of the fabric over by ½in and press. Turn this over by another ½in and pin in place along the quilted panel. Repeat along all the sides of the square and hand stitch in place all the way round. Press.

Dining Chair Cushion

This pretty chair cushion is made from nine blocks of fabric with alternate blocks made up of four small squares. Hand quilting has a charming quality and adds extra embellishment when done with colored embroidery thread. A frill finishes the cushion off beautifully, with the bottom edge left unhemmed as a decorative detail.

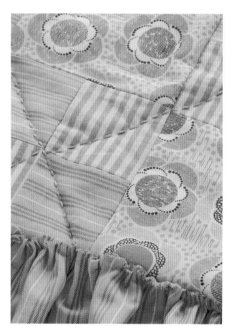

MATERIALS

12in square of two striped fabrics for the patchwork
8 x 46in strip of striped fabric for the frill
25½ x 6in of striped fabric for the ties
25½ x 6in piece of floral fabric
12½in square of striped fabric for the backing
12½in square of batting
Embroidery thread and needle

3 hours

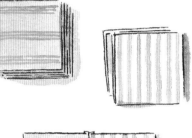

1. Measure and cut eight 2¾in squares of both of the two striped fabrics. With right sides together, pin and stitch one square of each together, and press the seams open.

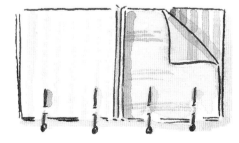

2. With right sides together, pin and stitch the two pieces from step 1 together, and press the seam open. Repeat this to make four patchwork squares.

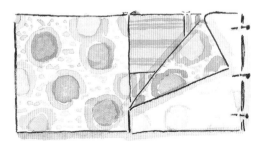

3. Using the flower fabric, measure and cut five 4¾in squares. Take one of these and with right sides together, join it to one of the patchwork squares. Stitch another flower fabric square to the other side of the patchwork square and press the seams open.

4. Make the central strip by joining two patchwork squares to either side of a flower fabric square in the same way as in step 3 and make the bottom strip as for the top. Join these three strips together to form a large square with alternating flower fabric and patchwork squares. Press the seams open.

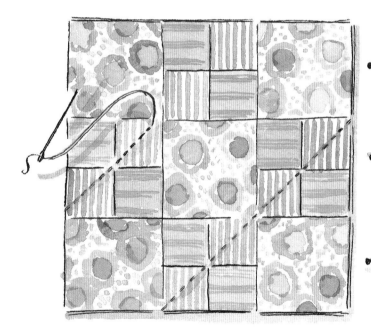

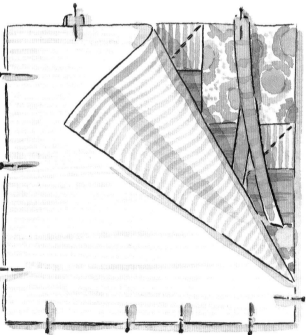

5. Cut a piece of batting 12⅝in square and place the patchwork on top of it. Pin the layers together. Using the embroidery thread, make a neat running stitch diagonally across the striped fabric squares.

6. Make the straps by cutting two 2 x 25in rectangles of one of the striped fabrics, folding them in half, and folding each side into the middle. Press and stitch. Fold these in half and place on the patchwork panel as indicated. Measure and cut a piece of one of the striped fabrics for the backing. Lay this on top of the patchwork with right sides together. Pin and stitch the layers together leaving an opening of about 6in along one side. Snip the corners and turn the right way out. Hand stitch the opening closed.

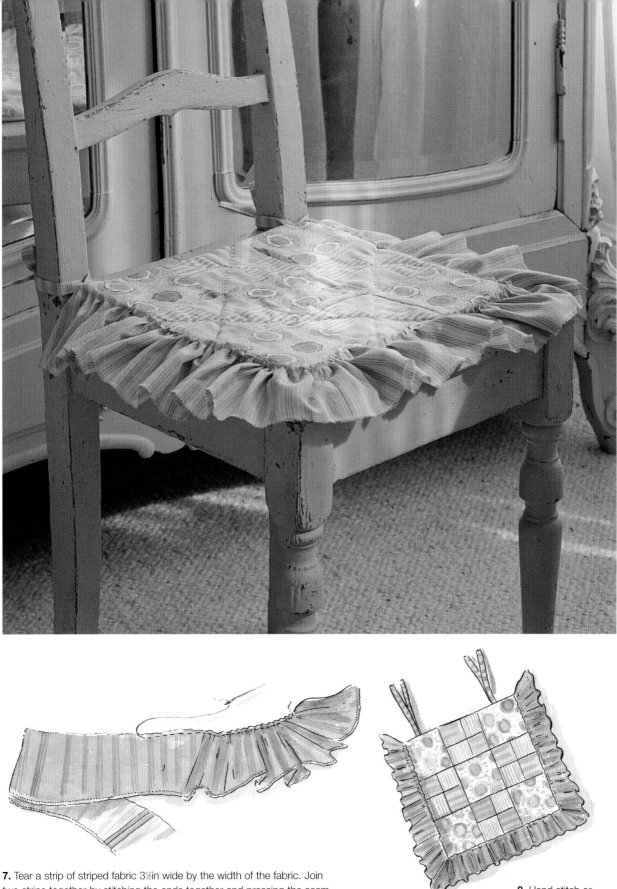

7. Tear a strip of striped fabric 3½in wide by the width of the fabric. Join two strips together by stitching the ends together and pressing the seam open to form a strip 80in long. Machine stitch along one side of it to prevent fraying. Make a running stitch along the other side of the strip and pull the thread to gather it so that it fits around the cushion. Sew a few stitches in the end to hold in place.

8. Hand stitch or machine stitch the frill round the cushion, turning either end under and hand stitching in place. Press carefully.

CHAPTER 3

Bedrooms

Shirting Fabric Throw

This quilt is so called because it is made from a selection of fine striped fabrics of the type often used for shirts. A central square turned on its side has been edged with triangles, which is then bordered with small squares and rectangles to create a regular pattern. The same fabric arrangements are repeated throughout the quilt.

MATERIALS

31½in square of fabric A
51 x 8in piece of fabric B
51 x 8in piece of fabric C
51 x 20in piece of fabric D
45½in square of backing fabric
Paper for pattern
45½in square cotton batting
9 buttons

←6 hours→

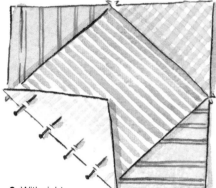

1. Cut out a piece of paper measuring 8¼in square. Use this to cut out nine squares from fabric A. Using the template on page 172, make a paper pattern for the triangle. Cut out 18 triangles in fabric B and 18 triangles in fabric C. With right sides together, pin and stitch two fabric B triangles onto opposite sides of a square. Press the seams away from the main square on the back. Repeat this using the other nine squares.

2. With right sides together, pin and stitch two triangles in fabric C onto the remaining sides of the squares. Again, press the seams away from the square.

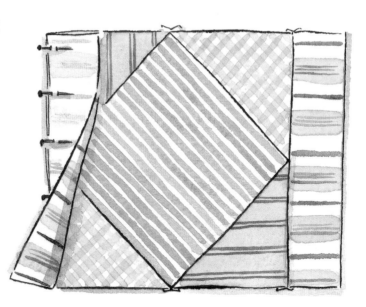

3. Cut a paper pattern rectangle 12 x 3⅛in. Use this to cut 18 strips of fabric D. Take two of these strips and with right sides together, pin and stitch them onto opposite sides of one of the patchwork squares. Press the seams open.

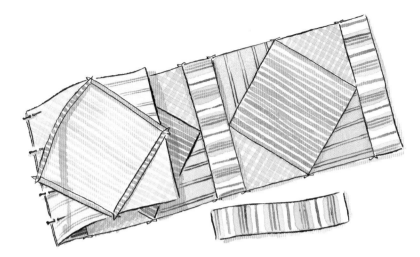

4. Pin and stitch a patchwork square onto this, with right sides together. Pin and stitch another strip to the other side of the square and continue until three patchwork squares are joined together with a strip of fabric D between each and one at each end. Keep all the squares the same way up (with fabric B at the left hand corner of each). Repeat this using the remaining six squares, to form three strips altogether.

5. Cut a paper pattern 3⅛in square. Use this to cut 16 squares of fabric A. Take one of these squares and pin and stitch it to the end of one of the D strips, with right sides together. Pin and stitch another square onto the other end. Repeat this to form a strip of three strips of fabric D with four squares of fabric A (one at each end). Press all the seams open.

6. With right sides together, pin and stitch one of the strips from step 5 along one long side of a patchwork panel. Press the seam open. Stitch another strip along the other side and again press the seam open. Pin and stitch another patchwork panel to this again with right sides together, and then another strip. Repeat this with the third patchwork panel finishing with the last long strip. Press the seams open and press the right side of the patchwork.

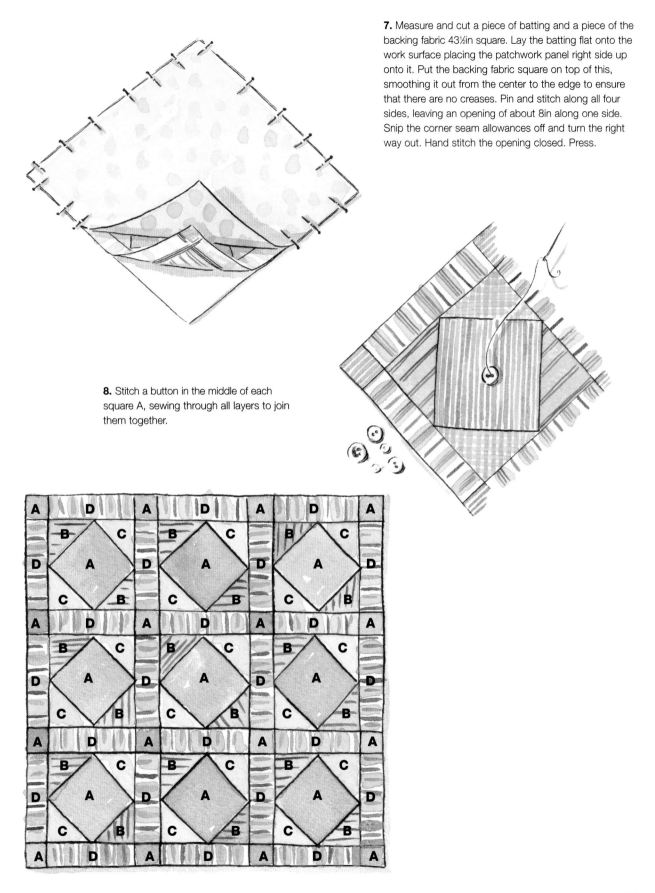

7. Measure and cut a piece of batting and a piece of the backing fabric 43½in square. Lay the batting flat onto the work surface placing the patchwork panel right side up onto it. Put the backing fabric square on top of this, smoothing it out from the center to the edge to ensure that there are no creases. Pin and stitch along all four sides, leaving an opening of about 8in along one side. Snip the corner seam allowances off and turn the right way out. Hand stitch the opening closed. Press.

8. Stitch a button in the middle of each square A, sewing through all layers to join them together.

1½ hours

MATERIALS

6 pieces of patterned fabric each measuring 13 x 14¼in
6 pieces of different fabrics each measuring 13 x 14¼in
4 strips of fabric each 13 x 41in
40 x 48in child's duvet
Felt flowers
Embroidery thread and needle

Quilt

This project is by far the simplest quilt in this book. Using a standard store-bought duvet as its base removes the need to cut a layer of batting and line up with backing fabric. A pretty patchwork cover is made from squares of fabric on one side, and stripes across the other, and is then filled with the duvet. It is quilted with sweet felt flowers, with knots to hold the layers together. Remove the felt flowers before machine-washing, or alternatively use buttons that can be left in place permanently.

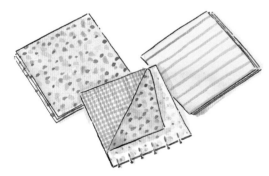

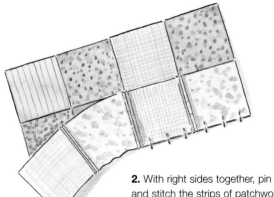

1. Cut out six pieces of patterned fabric measuring 13 x 14¼in. Cut six pieces of fabric in varying colours or patterns again measuring 13 x 14¼in. With right sides together, pin and stitch the squares together along their shorter sides, as illustrated, to make four strips of patchwork measuring 13 x 41in. Press the seams open.

2. With right sides together, pin and stitch the strips of patchwork together, lining up the seams neatly. Press the seams open to form the top of the quilt.

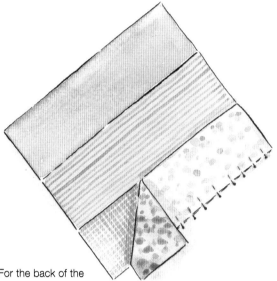

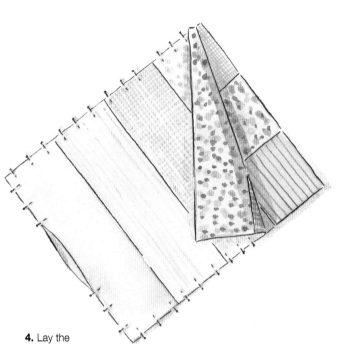

3. For the back of the quilt, cut another four strips of fabric measuring 13 x 41in. With right sides together, pin and stitch the strips together with a ½in seam. Press seams open.

4. Lay the patchwork panel right side up on the work surface ensuring that it is flat and crease free. Lay the back panel onto this with right sides together. Pin and stitch all the way round them leaving an opening of about 16in along one end. Snip the corner seam allowances off and turn the cover the right way out. Press.

5. Push the duvet inside the cover and straighten it out so that the corners of the duvet are pushed into the corners of the cover. Hand stitch the opening closed.

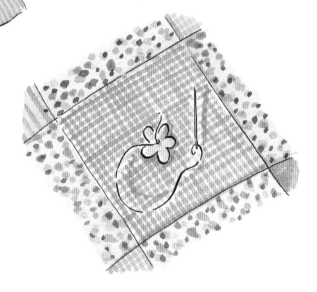

6. Using embroidery thread, sew a felt flower in the center of alternate patchwork squares. Leave the ends of the thread long and tie them into a firm knot.

Baby Crib Quilt

Babies' bedding doesn't need to be restricted to pastel colors. Here a bold print is teamed with stripes and spots to create a contemporary-looking crib quilt made from squares of fabric joined in strips. Remember to use lightweight batting, as young babies should not sleep under very thick covers.

3 hours

MATERIALS

20 x 36in main color fabric
8 x 36in of three different coordinating fabrics
Piece of gingham fabric at least 32½ x 28in for the backing
27 x 23in cotton batting
Embroidery thread and needle

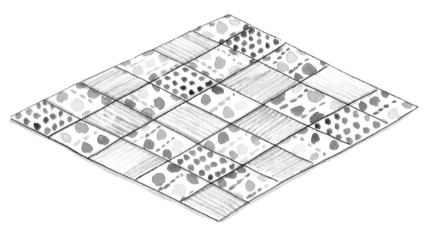

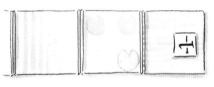

1. Cut a square paper pattern measuring 5½in. Cut out 15 squares of the main fabric, and five squares of each of the other three fabrics so that you have 30 squares in total. Arrange them on the work surface so that squares of the main fabric are laid out with three on the top line, two on the second line and so on, with squares of the other fabrics in between. There will be a block of five squares by six squares.

2. Pin a piece of paper onto the end of each line of squares, numbering them so that you will know their position. With right sides together, pin and stitch the squares together in their lines using a ½in seam and press the seams open.

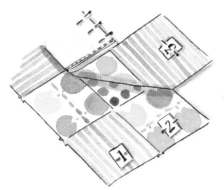

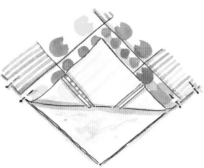

3. With right sides together, pin and stitch the strips together in the correct order using the numbers as the guide. Press the seams together.

4. Cut a piece of batting 28 x 23½in and lay the patchwork panel on top of it with right side up. Pin the layers together all round the edge.

5. Cut a piece of gingham fabric 32½ x 28in. Lay it onto the work surface (right side down if it has one). Place the batting and patchwork centrally on it ensuring that there is an even border all the way round. Turn a corner over by 2in and tuck the end under the batting.

6. Turn under ½in along one edge of the gingham fabric (pressing it if necessary) and then fold over and pin along the edge of the patchwork, covering the raw edge.

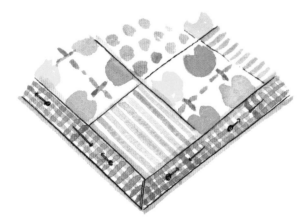

8. Hand stitch the border in place with small secure stitches. Take a length of about 16in of embroidery thread and, using a needle, stitch from the front to the back of the quilt at a corner point, leaving an end of thread about 4in long. Stitch back up through to the front of the quilt near where the needle first went through and repeat twice more, ending with the ends of the thread at the front. Tie the ends into a secure and neat knot and trim them to about 1¼in long. Repeat at each corner.

7. Repeat along all edges until all the border is pinned in place all around.

Duvet Cover

Duvet covers need to be made from very wide fabric that is not generally available from fabric stores in a good selection of interesting colors and patterns. Making a patchwork cover is the perfect solution; join squares of patterned and plain fabrics together to form one large panel the size that you need. Choose bold patterns mixed with a few plainer fabrics to create a contemporary patchwork design.

— 1½ hours —

MATERIALS

Enough fabric for 18 19in squares

83 x 90½in piece of fabric for the backing

Paper for template

1. Make a paper pattern 19in square. Use this to cut out 12 fabric squares from about five different fabrics. Fold the paper square in half to form a triangle. Use this to cut out 12 fabric triangles. Lay the squares and triangles out on a large flat surface following the illustration.

2. With right sides together, pin and stitch the triangles and squares together in each line. Press the seams open as you work.

3. Again with right sides together, pin and stitch the strips together to make one large panel, and press the seams open. Fold one side over to the wrong side by ⅛in and then by another ½in. Machine stitch along the hem and press.

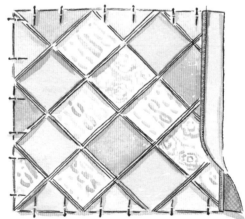

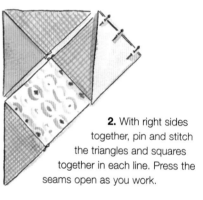

4. Measure and cut a piece of fabric the width of the patchwork panel by 90½in. Join two lengths together by stitching them with right sides together, pressing the seam open, and then cutting it to the right width if your fabric is not wide enough. Hem one end of it as in step 3. Lay the backing fabric flat onto the work surface right side up. Place the patchwork right side down onto it, lining up three edges exactly and making sure there are no creases or folds in either layer. Fold the excess fabric from the backing over to the wrong side of the patchwork. Pin and stitch along the other three sides of both layers. Snip the corners and turn the right way out, then press.

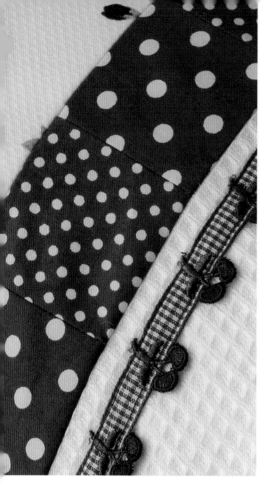

Pillowcase

Pillowcases are very easy to make. One of the nice things about making them yourself is that, with such a wide selection of fabrics available, they can be made in all sorts of lovely designs, a choice often lacking in store-bought bed linen. Here, a bright, floral fabric is used with a cheerful polka dot border and cherry trim. Having a whole set of bed linen in such a bright fabric would be a little overpowering, but a few pillowcases can liven up plain bed linen and add a more personal touch.

1½ hours

MATERIALS
16 x 4in pieces of two spotted fabrics
63 x 22in piece of floral fabric
22 x 16in piece of white fabric for the border
22in length of braid
3 ribbons
Paper for pattern

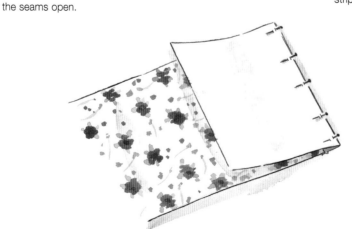

1. To make the patchwork strip, cut a paper pattern 2½in square. Pin onto both of the spotted fabrics and cut out five squares of each fabric. With right sides together, pin and stitch the squares together to form a long strip, alternating the different spotted fabrics. Press the seams open.

2. Measure and cut out a piece of floral fabric 20½ x 62in. With right sides together, pin and stitch the patchwork strip to one end of the floral strip. Press the seam toward the spotted fabric.

3. Measure and cut a piece of white fabric 20½ x 14¼in. With right sides together, pin and stitch this to the patchwork strip. Press the seam open.

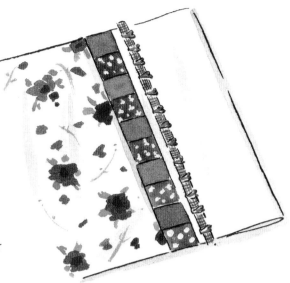

4. Fold the other side of the white fabric under ⅛in to the wrong side and press. With wrong side facing upward, line up the folded edge with the stitching line joining the floral fabric to the spotted patchwork strip. Pin and hand stitch in place.

5. With right side upward, take the braid and pin it to the white border about ½in from the spotted fabric strip. Machine stitch it in place, sewing along both edges of the braid.

6. Fold the raw edge of the floral fabric over to the wrong side by ½in and fold this over again by 1in. Pin and stitch ⅛in from the first fold. Press.

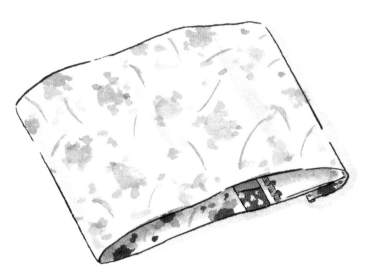

7. Lay the fabric panel onto the work surface right side up. Measure and make a fold 29½in from the edge of the white border fabric. Fold the fabric over the top with right sides together and fold the excess at the patchwork end underneath all the layers neatly. Pin and stitch along both sides. Turn the right way out and press.

Crazy Nine-patch Pillow

This pillow is made using a technique called crazy nine-patch and looks much more complicated than it is. Nine squares of different fabrics are cut and the layers mixed up to give you nine patchwork squares, each containing a block of all of the fabrics in different arrangements. It is great fun to make and produces a lovely effect, which could be used to produce a beautiful quilt when more blocks are made—or any number of other projects.

1 day

MATERIALS

8⅜in squares of each of nine different fabrics
10 x 28in piece of fabric for the border
28 x 43in piece of fabric for the backing
Metal ruler
Rotary cutter
25½in square pillow form

1. Lay the nine squares on top of each other making sure that they are exactly lined up. Take the rotary cutter and ruler and make a cut through all the layers at an angle as shown.

2. Take the top layer of the side strip and place it on the bottom of the pile. With right sides together, pin and stitch a main piece to the side strip next to it. Repeat with all nine layers, keeping them in order. Press the seams open.

3. Lay the nine squares exactly on top of each other in order. Using the rotary cutter and ruler again, make another cut on the left hand side of the square again at an angle, wider at the top than the bottom. Take the top two layers of the side strip and put them on the bottom of the pile. With right sides together, pin and stitch each side strip to the main piece next to it, pressing the seams open and keeping them in order.

4. With all the layers neatly stacked again, turn the pile around so that the seams run horizontally. Using the rotary cutter and ruler, make a third cut through all the layers at an angle so that the side strip is narrower at the top than the bottom. You may need to run the cutter along the line several times, to cut through all the fabric and seams.

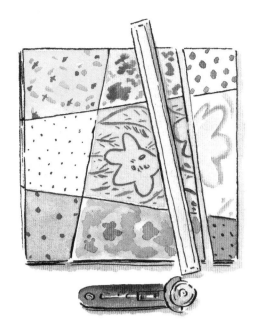

5. Take the top three layers of the side strip and put them at the bottom of the pile as before, and stitch each main piece to its side strip as before. Press the seams open.

6. Turn the pile of squares around again and cut a fourth strip with the top being wider than the bottom, as before. Take the top six layers and put them at the bottom of the pile. Sew both pieces from each layer together as before and press the seams open.

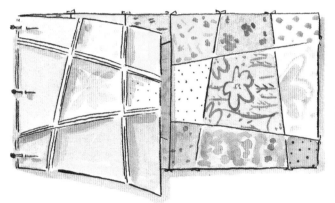

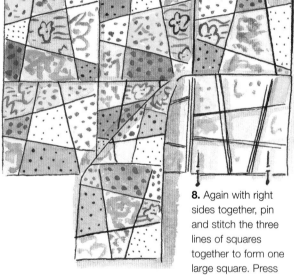

7. You will now have nine patchwork squares with a piece of each of the nine fabrics on each one. Trim each square to straighten up the sides and seams. Lay the squares in a block of three by three. With right sides together, pin and stitch the top three squares together, and repeat with the other two lines of three squares. Press the seams open.

8. Again with right sides together, pin and stitch the three lines of squares together to form one large square. Press the seams open.

9. Cut two strips of a coordinating fabric 2 x 23⅝in long. With right sides together, pin and stitch a strip onto two opposite sides of the patchwork square. Press the seams open.

10. Measure and cut two more strips of fabric 2 x 26⅝in long. Pin and stitch them onto the two remaining sides of the patchwork square, with right sides together. Press the seams open.

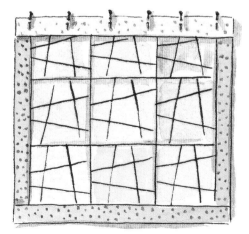

11. To make the back of the pillow, cut two rectangles of fabric measuring 26⅝ x 20in. Turn under ⅛in along one long side of both pieces and turn under another 1in. Pin and stitch along the first fold and press.

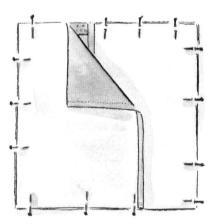

12. Lay the patchwork square right side up onto the work surface. Lay one of the back rectangles onto this right side down, matching up the raw edges. Lay the other rectangle on top of this with right side down, again matching up the raw edges. Pin and stitch all the way round the square. Snip the corner seam allowance off and turn the pillow cover the right way out. Press, and then fill with the pillow form.

Blue Quilt

The graphic look of this quilt is achieved by using classic checks and stripes with a bold solid color as the central block. Adding borders to a large central panel is a quick and easy way of creating a quilt and gives an eye-catching look that would work equally well on a sofa or armchair as on a bed.

1 day

MATERIALS

26in square of blue fabric for the center panel

31½ x 18in piece of checked fabric

39½ x 20in piece of striped fabric

46 x 18in piece of spotted fabric

46in square of fabric for backing

46in square of batting

Embroidery thread and needle

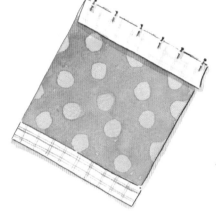

1. Measure and cut a central panel 24in square. Cut two strips of checked fabric 4 x 24in. With right sides together, pin and stitch the strips along opposite sides of the main panel. Press the seams open.

2. Measure and cut two more strips of checked fabric 4 x 32in. With right sides together, pin and stitch them along the other two sides of the main strip. Press the seams open.

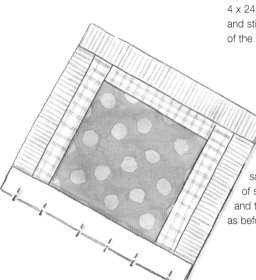

3. Cut two strips of striped fabric 4 x 32in, and two more strips 4 x 39in. Join them in the same way as before. Cut two strips of spotted fabric measuring 4 x 39in and two more of 4 x 46in, joining these as before.

4. Measure and cut a piece of batting and a piece of backing fabric 46in square. Lay the patchwork right side up onto the batting and the backing fabric with right side down onto this. Pin and stitch the three layers together all the way round leaving an opening of about 12in. Trim the corners and turn the right way out. Hand stitch the opening closed and press. Stitch knots at the corners of the strips to quilt it.

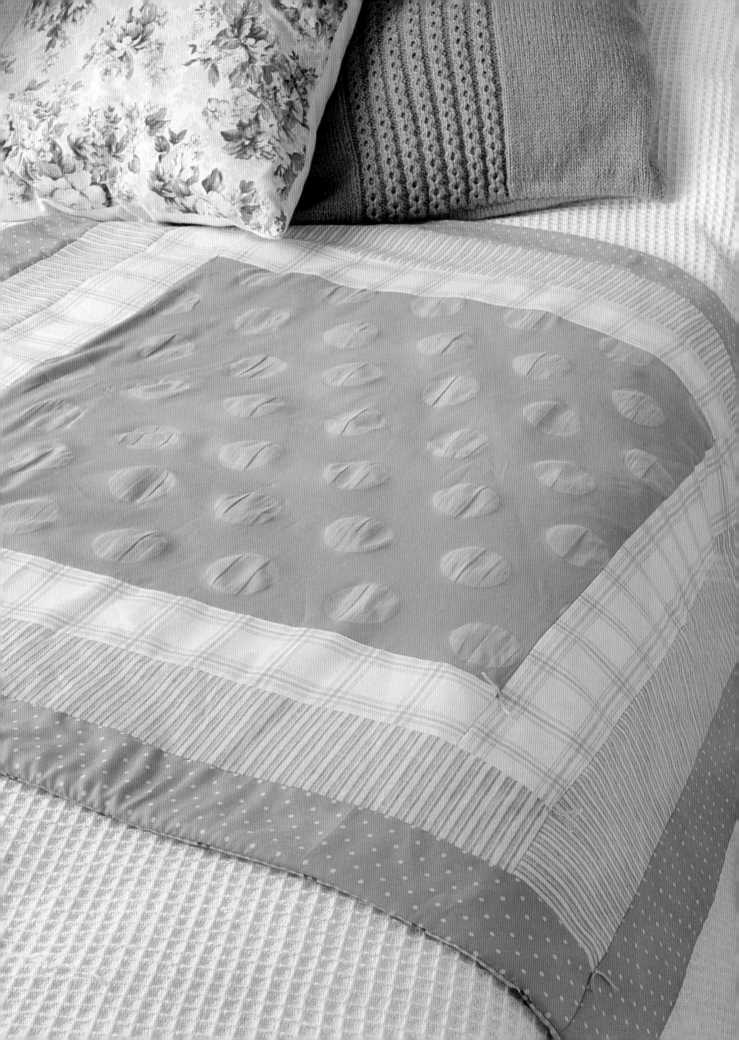

Pretty Quilt

5 hours

Patchwork has long been used as an economical way of producing beautiful home furnishings, using scraps of new and old fabrics. This charming quilt is made from squares of lots of different fabrics left over from other sewing projects, mixed with a plain linen fabric to unify the many patterns. Choosing fabrics with one or two colors in common will create a more harmonious effect, but the beauty of this design is that any fabric will work to create a lovely mismatched old-fashioned feel.

MATERIALS

6in squares of a mixture of patterned fabrics, 54 squares in total
36 x 54in piece of plain fabric
43 x 57in piece of batting
12 x 57in piece of fabric for the binding
43 x 57in piece of fabric for the backing
Embroidery thread and needle
Paper for the markers

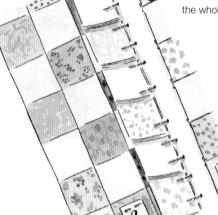

1. Cut a 5in square paper pattern. Using this, cut out 54 squares of plain fabric and 54 squares of patterned fabrics. Arrange them on the work surface, alternating plain and patterned squares until you are happy with the arrangement.

2. With right sides together, pin and stitch the squares together, working from left to right vertically to form 12 strips of nine squares. Press the seams open, and label each strip with a number (pinning paper to the bottom of each) to keep the correct order.

3. With right sides together, pin and stitch the strips together, working from the left to the right hand side. Press the seams open as you go. Remove the numbers and press the whole patchwork panel.

4. Measure and cut a piece of wadding 54 x 40 ½in and a piece of backing fabric the same size. Lay the backing fabric wrong side up on the work surface and put the batting on top of this. Lay the patchwork panel on top of this, smoothing it out to remove any creases.

5. Measure and cut a strip of binding fabric 2 x 190in. Join strips together if necessary by stitching the ends together with right sides together, pressing the seams open. Press under ½in at one end and pin the strip to the patchwork, lining up the raw edges. Ease the fabric round the corners, making a small pleat. Machine stitch in place, overlapping the ends.

6. Snip the corners off. Press under ½in along the remaining raw edge of the binding strip. Pin this folded edge onto the back of the quilt and hand stitch in place.

CHAPTER 4

Work & Play Spaces

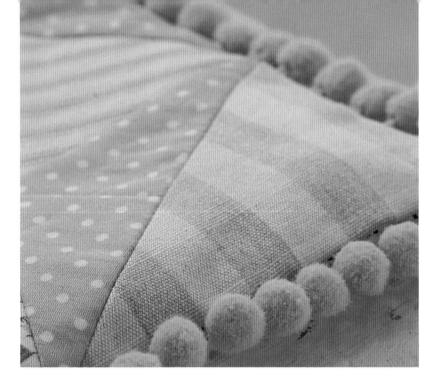

3 hours

Child's Seat Cushion

Making a cushion for a simple wooden chair can add a lovely decorative touch. This patchwork star is a slightly more complex design, but can easily be made using a sewing machine. It can be made to fit any size of seat by increasing the size of the templates accordingly. A cute bobble fringe finishes the cushion off beautifully, with fabric ties added to hold it in place.

1. Using the template on page 169, cut out pattern pieces A, B, and C. Cut out three pieces of A from each of the two different fabrics. Cut out 12 pieces of B in one fabric. With right sides together, pin and stitch one B piece along one edge of an A piece. Press the seam open. Stitch another B piece along the next side of the A piece and again press the seam open. Continue joining two B pieces to each of the six A pieces.

2. With right sides together, pin and stitch three of the shapes made in step 1 together, alternating the different fabrics to form two semicircles. Press all the seams open.

3. Again with right sides together, pin and stitch these two pieces together, and press the seam open. Trim off any bits of seam allowance that stick out round the edge.

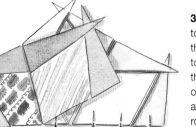

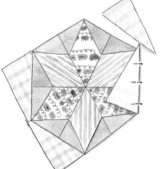

4. Lay the patchwork star onto the work surface with one of its points at the top. Using pattern piece C, cut four triangles from the checked fabric. With right sides together, pin and stitch them onto the top and bottom corners of the star. Press the seams open.

5. Measure and cut two 1½ x 18in strips of one of the fabrics. Fold them both in half along their length and press. Fold the edges into the center fold and press. Pin and stitch along the length of both to form the ties.

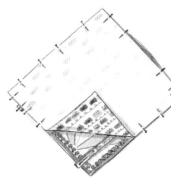

6. Cut a piece of backing fabric the same size as the patchwork panel. Pin and baste the bobble fringe all the way round the right side of the patchwork panel, with the bobbles pointing inward. Fold the ties in half and position them at the top of the patchwork panel an inch or so from both top corners. Place the backing fabric right sides together onto the patchwork and pin and stitch all the way round, leaving an opening of about 4in along the top edge. Turn the right way out. Cut a piece of batting to fit the cover and push in place. Hand stitch the opening closed. Press.

Play Mat

Six different fabrics have been used to make this baby's play mat. Polka dots and checks in similar colors create a harmonious look that is as practical as it is attractive. With a patchwork-pieced star at the center, it is built up with strips of fabric around the sides and squares at the corners. Use a synthetic batting (or cotton batting that is machine washable) so that the mat can be laundered regularly.

⟨1½ hours⟩

MATERIALS

23 x 8in piece of fabric A
12 x 20in piece of fabric B
12 x 23½in piece of fabric C
12in square of fabric D
18 x 23½in piece of fabric E
23½ x 35½in piece of fabric F
35½in square of fabric for backing
35½in square of heavy-weight batting
Paper for pattern pieces

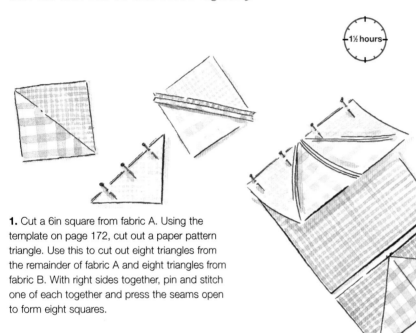

1. Cut a 6in square from fabric A. Using the template on page 172, cut out a paper pattern triangle. Use this to cut out eight triangles from the remainder of fabric A and eight triangles from fabric B. With right sides together, pin and stitch one of each together and press the seams open to form eight squares.

2. With right sides together, pin and stitch two of the squares together with the two triangles of fabric B next to each other. Repeat this with the other squares to form four rectangles. Press the seams open. Take two of the rectangles and pin and stitch them onto opposite sides of the A fabric square from step 1. Press the seams open.

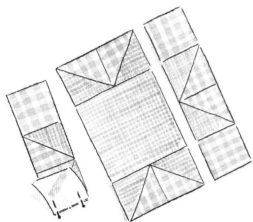

3. Using fabric B again, cut four 3¼in squares. Pin and stitch two of them onto each end of the two remaining rectangles with right sides together. Press the seams open. Again with right sides together, pin and stitch these strips onto the two remaining raw sides of the central square, matching up the seams. Press the seams open.

4. Measure and cut four 4 x 10½in rectangles of fabric C and pin and stitch two of them onto opposite sides of the patchwork panel with right sides together.

5. Cut four 4in squares of fabric D and stitch them onto the ends of the remaining two strips of fabric C, with right sides together. Press the seams open. Pin and stitch these onto the other two sides of the patchwork panel, pressing the seams open.

6. Take fabric E and measure and cut four strips 4¾ x 17½in. Pin and stitch two of them onto opposite sides of the patchwork and press the seams open. Cut four 4¾in squares of fabric B and pin and stitch them onto each end of the remaining two strips of fabric E. Press the seams open and pin and stitch them onto the patchwork panel.

7. Using fabric F measure and cut two strips 4¾ x 26in. With right sides together, pin and stitch them onto opposite sides of the patchwork panel and press all the seams open. Cut two more 4¾ x 34½in strips of fabric F and pin and stitch them onto the patchwork panel, then press all the seams open.

8. Cut 34½in squares of batting and backing fabric. Lay the patchwork on the batting right side up and place the backing fabric on top of this, smoothing out all the layers as you go. Pin and stitch all the way round leaving an opening of about 12in along one side. Snip the corners and turn the right way out. Hand stitch the opening closed and press. Machine stitch along the seams to quilt through all the layers. Press.

Child's Pillow

This pretty patchwork pillow is perfect for a girl's bedroom. Three fabrics are pieced together to form a square, which is then backed with batting and quilted to make an even softer cushion. The decorative trim is made from strips of unhemmed fabric, gathered and stitched along the seams, with a fabric rosette to finish.

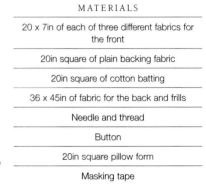

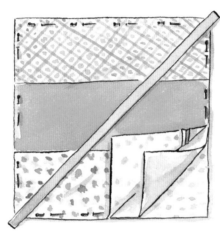

6 hours

MATERIALS
20 x 7in of each of three different fabrics for the front
20in square of plain backing fabric
20in square of cotton batting
36 x 45in of fabric for the back and frills
Needle and thread
Button
20in square pillow form
Masking tape

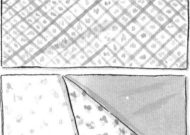

1. Measure and cut three rectangles of different fabrics 20 x 7in. With right sides together, pin and stitch them together along the long sides to form a square. Press the seams open.

2. Cut a piece of fabric and a piece of batting 20in square. Lay the backing fabric right side down on the work surface with the batting on top. Place the patchwork panel right side up onto this and smooth out all the layers. Pin the layers together. Stick masking tape from one corner to the opposite corner and stitch along one side of it.

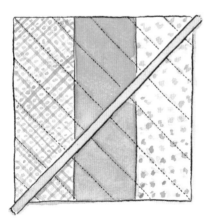

3. Continue to stick masking tape onto the fabric, spacing each strip 3¼in from the previous stitch line and stitching along it, until you reach each corner. Then repeat this process working from the other corners so that the panel is quilted.

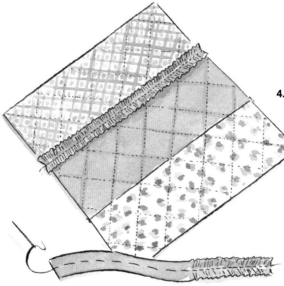

4. Tear a strip of fabric 1½in wide by the width of the fabric you are using and make a running stitch centrally along its length. Gather the strip and pin along one of the seams on the patchwork. Make another gathered strip for the other seam. Machine stitch the gathered strips in place.

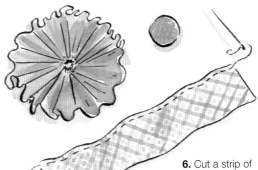

5. Measure and cut two pieces of fabric 20 x 16in. Fold over ½in along one long side and fold this over by another ¾in to the wrong side to hem it. Pin and machine stitch. Place one of these pieces with right sides together onto the patchwork panel, lining up the three raw edges. Place the second hemmed fabric piece and place this over the top with right side down, lining up the three raw edges. Pin and stitch all the way round the cover. Snip the corners and turn the right way out.

6. Cut a strip of one of the front fabrics 20 x 2in. Make a running stitch along one side of it and gather to form a rosette shape. Cut a smaller piece of the back fabric 16 x 1½in and do the same, then stitch the two together, sewing a button in the middle. Sew onto the pillow cover, adding a few strips of fabric hanging down for extra decoration. Fill the cover with the pillow form.

Toy Bag

Drawstring bags are great for storing toys in and can be hung up out of the way at the end of the day. This bold print has been enhanced with a pretty patchwork panel edged in a chunky rickrack braid. These bags don't need to be restricted to just toys—they can be made in any size to house all sorts of things from laundry, clothes and shoes to toiletries and cosmetics, by altering the dimensions to the size required.

6 hours

MATERIALS

32 x 40in piece of main fabric for bag
16 x 12in pieces of each of two fabrics for patchwork
12 x 24in piece of fabric for the top lining
8 x 24in piece of gingham fabric
44in length of rickrack
99in length of ribbon
Safety pin

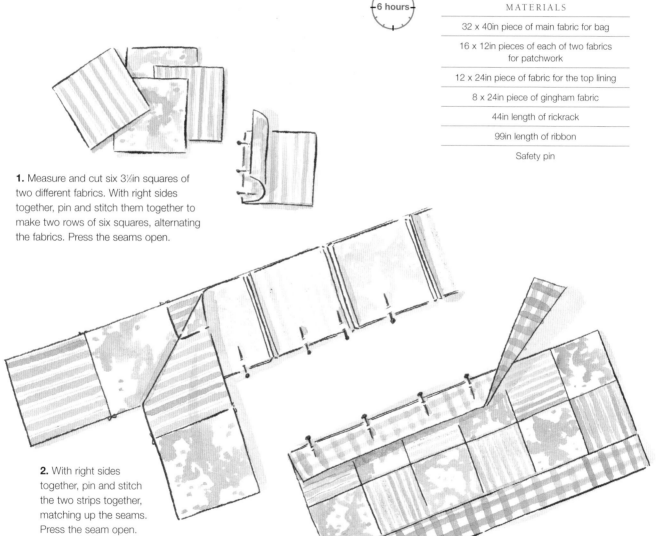

1. Measure and cut six 3½in squares of two different fabrics. With right sides together, pin and stitch them together to make two rows of six squares, alternating the fabrics. Press the seams open.

2. With right sides together, pin and stitch the two strips together, matching up the seams. Press the seam open.

3. Measure and cut two strips of gingham 1¾ x 22in. With right sides together, pin and stitch them onto either side of the patchwork panel. Press the seams open.

4. Take the main flower fabric and cut one rectangle 6½ x 22in and then another one 15 x 18½in. With right sides together, pin and stitch them onto either side of the patchwork panel and press the seams open.

5. Cut two pieces of ticking 4½ x 22in. Place one of them with right sides together onto the top of the front panel and pin and stitch across the top and down each side 2¾in from the top. Snip the corners. Sew rickrack across the top and bottom of the patchwork, and trim the ends.

6. Cut a piece of the main flower fabric 29½ x 22in. Pin and stitch the second piece of ticking to the top of it as in step 5 with right sides together. Pin and stitch the front of the bag to the back with right sides together, starting and stopping the stitching 4in from the top edge. Snip the corners and turn the right way out.

7. Fold ¼in under along both sides and the bottom edge on both pieces of ticking fabric panels and pin and top stitch onto the front and back of the bag, sewing near to the bottom fold. Make another stitch line 1¼in up from this on the front and the back to form a channel.

8. Thread a safety pin through the end of the ribbon and feed it through the channel on the front and back of the bag and tie the ends in a knot at one side. Thread another length of ribbon through from the other side front and back again and again tie the ends in a knot, on the other side. Pull both ribbons to gather up the bag. Sew a loop of ribbon to the back of the bag to hang it up.

Baby's Ball

This is a great gift for a newborn and is easy to do. Choose fabrics with a small print, or try large, bold bright fabrics to really catch a baby's eye. When making items for children, a good starting point for fabrics can be children's clothes that have been outgrown, as they are often in small prints that work well for projects like this. The ball is filled with synthetic stuffing so that it is machine washable. Place a bell in the middle as you stuff, to keep the baby well entertained.

2 hours

MATERIALS

Assorted scraps of fabric to cut into 5in pentagons

Stiff paper for the backing

Needle and thread

Stuffing

Bell

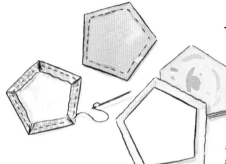

1. Using the template on page 168, cut out 12 backing papers using the stiff paper. Pin them onto the wrong side of the fabric and cut out, adding an extra ⅛in all the way round to make 12 pentagons. Fold over the ⅛in of the fabric onto the paper and baste in position. Repeat with all 12 paper backed pentagons.

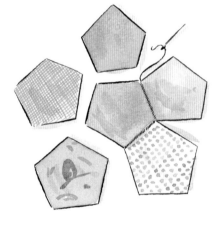

2. Lay one of the pentagons right side up on the work surface and arrange five of the others around it. With right sides together, whipstitch each edge together. Repeat with the remaining six pentagons.

3. Join the two sets of six pentagons together in the same way, whipstitching along all the edges together to form a sphere. Leave one side open.

4. Remove the basting stitches from each pentagon and remove the backing papers. Turn the ball the right way out. Stuff the ball, packing the stuffing in to create a good shape and adding a bell in the middle. Hand stitch the opening closed.

Knitting Bag

Every crafter needs a knitting bag to hold balls of wool and knitting needles, but many commercially available versions are more practical than decorative. This stylish bag is roomy enough to hold plenty of wool and looks good as well. Interfacing has been used to make the fabric as stiff as possible so that it holds its shape, and all the layers are quilted to create a sturdy bag.

MATERIALS

30 x 15in piece of patterned fabric

40 x 12in plain white cotton

40 x 12in piece of cotton batting

40 x 14in piece of plain colored fabric

Masking tape

Iron-on interfacing

2 buttons

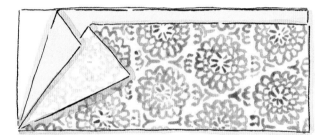

1. Measure and cut a piece of white cotton and a piece of batting 30 x 12in. Measure and cut a rectangle of patterned fabric 30 x 11in. Lay the white cotton onto the work surface with the batting on top of this. Place the patterned fabric rectangle, right side up, onto this, lining up the bottom edges together. Pin layers together.

2. Stick a strip of masking tape vertically from the bottom to the top of the fabrics. Measure 1½in from the left hand side of the tape, sticking another strip of tape parallel to the first. Continue at 1½in increments, measuring from the left hand side of the tape all the way along the fabric. Machine stitch along the left hand side of each length of tape to quilt the fabric.

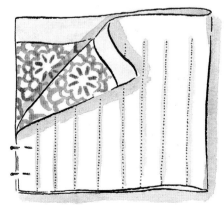

3. With patterned fabric right sides together, fold the panel over, lining up along both short sides. Pin and stitch along the edge, and press the seam open.

4. Cut circles of white cotton, cotton batting and patterned fabric, all with a diameter of 9½in. Lay the white cotton onto the work surface with the batting on top of this. Place the patterned fabric circle on the top, right side up. Pin the layers together. Stick a length of tape across the circle and measure and stick parallel strips on either side of the first at 1½in increments as before, across the width of the circle. Machine stitch along one side of each length of tape.

5. Measure and cut a piece of the plain colored fabric 30 x 13½in. With right sides together (if there is a right and wrong side), pin and stitch both short sides together. Place this over the quilted tube, right side out, with the top raw edge lining up with the raw edge of the patterned fabric. Pin and stitch the plain fabric onto the quilted tube.

6. With right sides together, pin and stitch the circular base to the main part of the bag. Turn the bag the right way out and push the lining inside. Press the top edge of the lining to form a neat edge. Top stitch around the top and bottom of the cuff.

7. Cut a circle of plain colored fabric for the base of the lining the same size as before. Turn the bag wrong side out again. With right sides together if applicable, pin and stitch the base to the main lining piece, leaving an opening of about 4in. Make small snips around the seam allowance and turn the bag the right way out through the gap in the lining. Hand stitch the opening in the lining closed and push the lining into the bag.

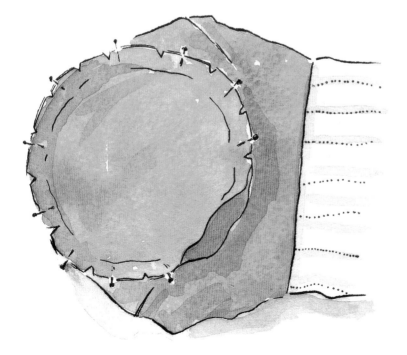

8. Cut a strip of patterned fabric 23 x 4in. Cut a piece of interfacing to the same size and, following the manufacturer's directions, attach it to the wrong side of the fabric strip. Fold the strip in half along its length and stitch along one short end and along the length. Snip the corners. Turn the tube the right way out and press. Turn the raw end in and top stitch all the way round the handle. Sew the handle onto the bag finishing with a button at each end of it.

Sewing Basket

A plain store-bought basket can easily be transformed into a charming sewing basket large enough to store a complete sewing kit. Diamond-shaped patches are pieced together to form a long strip that is then used to line the basket, with a smaller panel of the same patchwork padded and fixed to the underside of the lid to create an in situ pincushion.

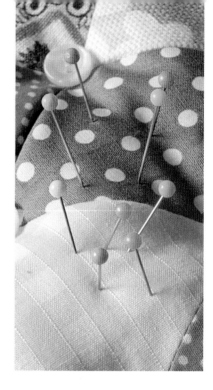

MATERIALS
Large selection of assorted fabric scraps for the diamonds
Basket with lid
Piece of fabric slightly bigger than the basket base
2in strip of a full width of fabric for the binding
Piece of lining fabric slightly bigger than basket lid
Piece of medium-weight batting slightly bigger than basket lid
Paper for pattern
12 buttons (approx.)
Needle and thread
Fast drying high-tack adhesive

5 hours

1. Using the template on page 172, cut out a diamond-shaped pattern. Use this to cut out diamond shapes in lots of different fabrics. To join the diamonds together, pin and stitch them with right sides together to form a strip. Press the seams open.

2. For this basket, I have used strips of five diamonds long; for a different size basket alter this accordingly. Continue to make strips of diamonds and then join them together with right sides together to form a panel. Keep adding strips until the panel is long enough to fit around the inside walls of the basket with a ½in seam allowance at each end, and deep enough to fold over the top edge. Make shorter strips at each end to make a rectangle shape. Press all the seams open as you go.

3. Using a pair of scissors, cut off the triangles across the top and bottom of the panel to make a rectangle and discard the offcuts. Fit the rectangle inside the basket and trim if necessary so that it sits snugly inside, adding the seam allowance at either end. Press the rectangle.

4. Fold the rectangle over with right sides together and pin and stitch down the side. Press the seam open.

5. Measure and cut a piece of fabric for the bottom liner to fit the bottom of the basket plus ½in seam allowance along each side. With right sides together, pin and stitch the patchwork sides to the base. Trim the corners and press.

6. Cut a piece of one of the fabrics 1½in wide and long enough to go around the edge of the basket liner plus a seam allowance at each end. With right sides together, pin and stitch binding around the basket liner, turning under the ends neatly and overlapping them slightly. Turn under ½in along the raw edge of the binding and fold it over to the back of the basket liner and hand stitch in place. Press and put into the basket, folding the edge over the top.

7. To make the pincushion for the lid, measure inside the lid and make a rectangle of diamond patchwork fabric to fit, adding ⅝in to each side. Cut a piece of lining fabric the same size as the patchwork rectangle and with right sides together, pin and stitch the rectangles together using a ½in seam allowance and leaving an opening of about 2in along one side. Snip the corners, turn the right way out, and press.

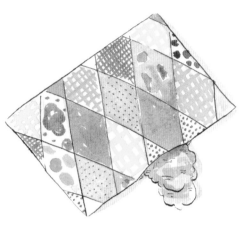

8. Cut a piece of batting to fit and put inside, pushing it into the corners. Hand stitch the opening closed.

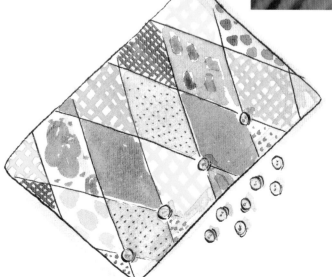

9. Hand stitch buttons onto the intersections of the diamonds, sewing through all the layers to quilt them. When all the buttons have been sewn on, glue the cushion inside the lid of the basket, pressing it in place firmly until the glue is dry.

Pincushion

Every crafter needs a pincushion and this sweet version really does require nothing but the smallest of scraps of fabric to make. Constructed from two circles of patchwork segments, it is tightly stuffed so that it will safely keep pins and needles in place, and has a pretty rosette and button to make it decorative as well as practical.

⊕ 1 hour

MATERIALS

Scraps of fabric

Paper for pattern

Stuffing

Embroidery thread and needle

Decorative button

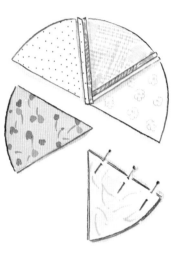

1. Using the template on page 171, cut out six segment pieces for the top of the pincushion and six for the bottom from scraps of several different fabrics. Lay them onto the work surface and move them around until you are happy with the arrangement.

2. With right sides together, pin and stitch three of the segment pieces together. Repeat with the other three pieces of fabric and press all the seams open.

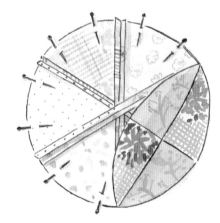

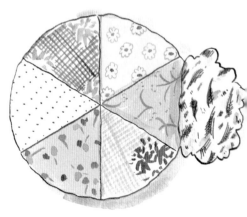

3. With right sides together, pin and stitch the two semicircles together along their straight edge. Press the seam open. Repeat steps 2 and 3 using the fabric segments for the bottom of the pincushion.

4. With right sides together, pin and stitch the two fabric circles together, lining up the fabric joins on the top and bottom pieces. Leave an opening of about 1in. Make small snips all the way round in the seam allowance and turn the cushion the right way out. Press.

5. Fill the cushion with stuffing, pushing it through the opening and working it evenly all around the cushion. Use a pencil or knitting needle to push the stuffing in, if necessary. When it is nicely padded, hand stitch the opening closed.

6. Take a length of embroidery thread and tie a knot in the end. Push the needle through the center of the top of the cushion and pull through the bottom. Bring the needle back to the top and push it back through the center, pulling the thread so that it lines up with a fabric join. Pull quite tight and continue until there is a line of thread along each fabric join. Finish with a few stitches at the center.

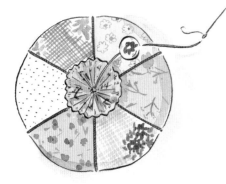

7. Using the template on page 171, cut a circle of fabric and make a running stitch all the way round the edge (about ⅛in in). Pull the thread, gathering the fabric to form a small yo-yo. Finish with a few stitches.

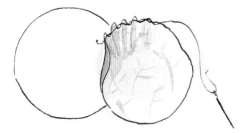

8. Sew the yo-yo onto the center of the top of the cushion, finish by stitching on a button, then push the needle back through the cushion to the underside and fasten off with a few stitches.

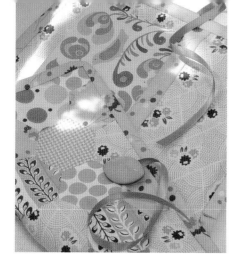

Notebook Folder

This charming stationery folder is one of the few projects in this book that is hand rather than machine stitched. Don't let that put you off though, as sewing these hexagon patches together may take slightly longer than machine sewing a patchwork panel, but it is an incredibly relaxing and enjoyable activity that produces really beautiful patchwork at the end. This folder has been made to hold pencils and a notebook, ideal for sketching trips or using to note ideas for other craft projects when you are out and about. Try making a longer, narrower version to hold knitting needles, or vary the widths of the pockets to hold all your sewing tools.

6 hours

MATERIALS

Scraps of fabric to cut 28 hexagons

Paper for patchworking

7½ x 10in piece of fabric to coordinate with patchwork

15 x 17in piece of fabric for the lining

50½ x 4in piece of contrast fabric for binding

15 x 10in piece of batting

12in length of ribbon for the tie

Large button

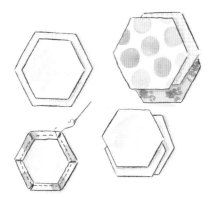

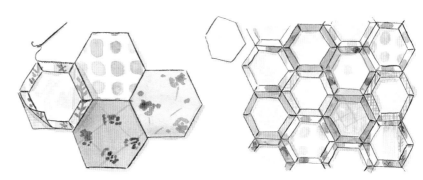

1. Using the larger hexagon template on page 171, cut out 28 hexagons from fabric. Using the smaller hexagon template, cut out 28 paper shapes. Place a paper shape onto the back of a fabric hexagon and press the edges of the fabric over the paper using a cool iron. Using a needle and thread, baste around the hexagon through the paper and finish with a few small stitches. Repeat for all 28 fabric hexagons.

2. Arrange the fabric hexagons onto the work surface in alternate rows of six and five rows until you are happy with the arrangement. With right sides together and using a needle and thread, start to stitch the hexagon patches together by overcasting the edges.

3. Continue stitching all the patches together until you have a panel of patches. Unpick the basting stitches and remove the backing papers. Trim the patches to make a neat rectangle measuring 7½ x 10in. Press. Cut a piece of coordinating fabric 7½ x 10in and with right sides together, stitch it to one of the longer sides of the patchwork. Press the seam open.

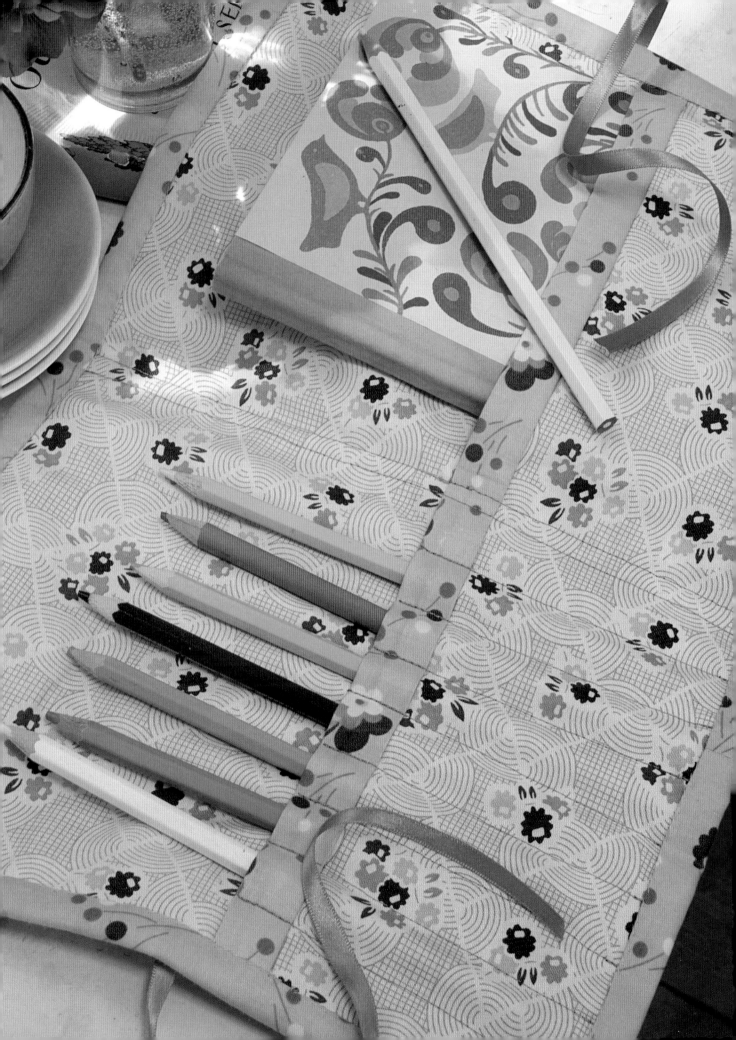

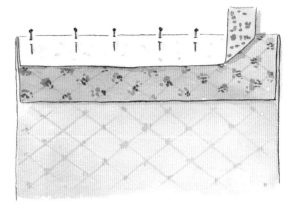
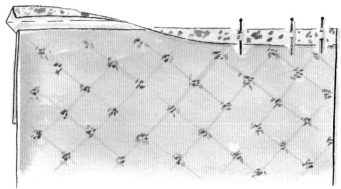

4. Measure and cut a rectangle of lining fabric 15 x 17in long. Lay it right side down onto the work surface and fold over 4in to the wrong side at the top. Cut a strip of binding fabric 15 x 2in. With right sides together, pin the strip along the fold at the top of the rectangle and stitch through all the layers using the ½in seam allowance.

5. Press ½in to the wrong side along the strip of fabric. Turn the large rectangle of fabric over right side up. Fold the strip of fabric over the folded edge of the large rectangle and pin in place. Hand stitch the fold of the strip onto the fabric rectangle. Press. Fold the double layer section of the rectangle over right sides together, so that the coordinating strip is 4½in from the bottom and the fold line you make lines up with the raw edge at the bottom. This forms the pocket.

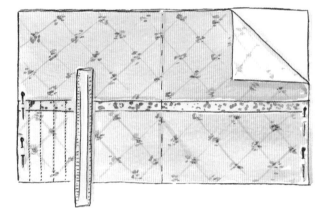

6. Cut a piece of batting 15 x 10in. Lay the lining fabric (with the pocket) right side up on top of it and pin all the way round the outside to hold the layers together. Measure and mark with masking tape a line centrally from the top to the bottom of the fabric. Stitch along this line. Using masking tape as your guide, stitch from the top to the bottom of the pocket at ⅞in intervals to make the pencil pockets.

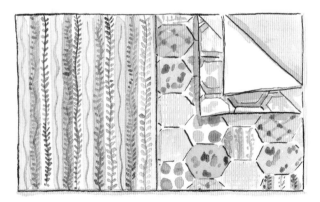
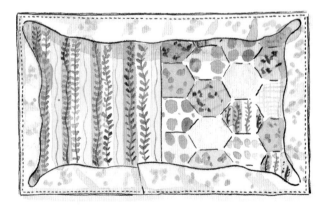

7. Lay the lining right side down and place the patchwork panel right side up onto it. Pin down the center and machine stitch along the join of the fabrics to join all the layers together, making sure your line of stitching is in the same position as the central line made in step 6.

8. Cut a strip of binding fabric 2 x 50½in long. Fold one end to the wrong side and press. Pin onto the right side of the front of the folder, easing it round the corners neatly. Overlap the ends slightly and trim off any excess fabric. Machine stitch the fabric in place. Trim the corners slightly.

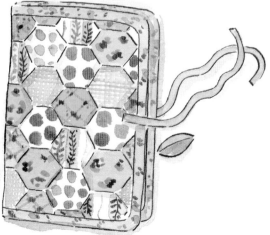

9. Press ⅛in to the wrong side on the remaining raw edge of the binding. Turn it over to the inside of the folder and hand stitch in place all the way round. Finish the folder with two lengths of ribbon stitched to the front and back of the folder half way along the outer edge. Sew a large button onto the front.

Gardening Apron

Choose heavy-weight fabrics for this gardening apron, which is made even sturdier by adding a layer of batting and quilting all the layers together. Handy pockets can hold seed packets, twine, and plant markers and there are loops stitched across the apron to keep tools close at hand while out in the garden. Make the ties long enough to tie twice around your waist to hold it securely in place when you wear it.

MATERIALS

30 x 22in pieces of two different fabrics for the main apron

87 x 12in for the ties and pocket strap

30 x 22in piece of light-weight batting

1½ hours

1. Measure and cut two rectangles of fabric and one of the batting 19½ x 28½in. Place the floral fabric onto the batting right side up and lay the ticking right side down onto it. Pin and stitch around the sides and bottom. Snip the corners and turn the right way out.

2. Measure and mark five lines 1½in apart, horizontally from the bottom up across the panel, using pins or masking tape. Machine stitch along each line to quilt the panel.

3. To make the pocket strap, cut a piece of the ticking fabric 2½ x 28½in. Fold it in half along its length and press. Fold both sides into the middle fold and pin and stitch along its length. Press.

4. Lay the pocket strap across the quilted panel about ¾in from the edge. Pin and stitch it at 3½in from the left and right hand sides and with another stitch line 3in from one of these stitch lines.

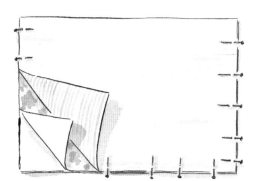

5. Fold the quilted panel to form a pocket 8in deep. Machine stitch along both ends folding the pocket strap into the seam. Stitch down the pocket from the top to the bottom to form pockets.

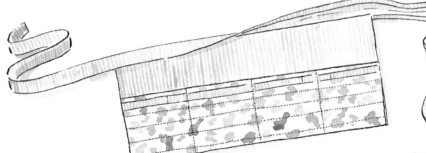

6. To make the ties, cut a strip of ticking 2½ x 87in (join two lengths if necessary by stitching the ends together with right sides together and pressing the seam open). Find the middle of the strip and lay it along the top of the apron, centrally on the back. Machine stitch the two together. Press under ⅛in along both sides of the ties to the wrong side and fold over to the front of the apron. Pin in place and along the length of the ties, folding both ends in to the wrong side also. Top stitch along the length and both ends. Press.

CHAPTER 5

Laundry & Bathrooms

3 hours

Clothes Pin Bag

The punchy color combination of this clothes pin bag will brighten up the dullest of washing days. Strips of patterned fabrics are teamed with a plain fabric to make the front panel, which has been decorated with ribbon and braid. The strap clips onto the bag with a snap fastener, enabling it to be hung on the line when hanging out the washing, and it is roomy enough to hold plenty of clothes pins.

MATERIALS

12 x 20in pieces of three coordinating fabrics for the front
18in square of fabric for the back
36 x 18in piece of fabric for lining
Paper for pattern
16in of rickrack
16in of ribbon
20 x 8in iron-on interfacing
Sturdy snap
Large button
Needle and thread

1. Cut strips of the three fabrics 18in long and in various widths from 4in to 1½in. With right sides together, pin and stitch the strips together, pressing the seams open as you work. The finished panel of patchwork needs to be at least 15 x 18in.

2. Using the template on page 171, make a paper pattern. Pin onto the patchwork panel and cut out.

3. Pin and stitch rickrack and ribbon along some of the seams, randomly. Trim the ends to neaten them.

4. Using the paper pattern again, pin it onto a piece of fabric and cut out for the back of the bag. With right sides together, pin and stitch the back piece to the front patchwork piece along both sides and the bottom. Turn the right way out.

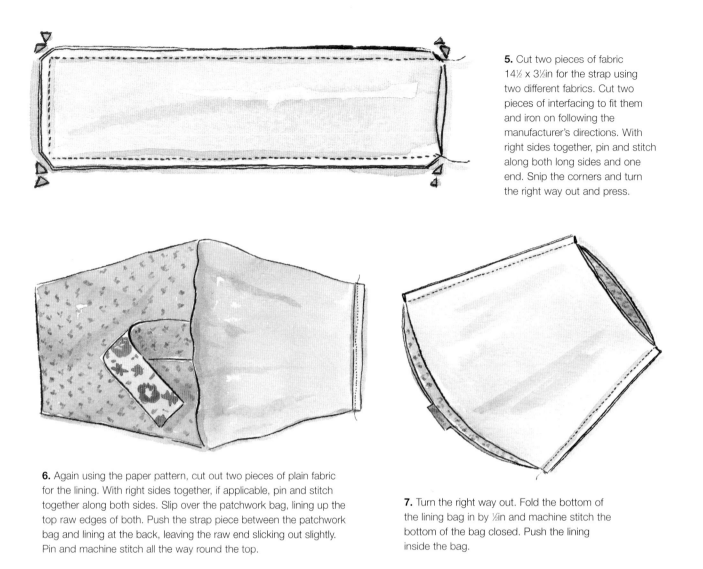

5. Cut two pieces of fabric 14½ x 3½in for the strap using two different fabrics. Cut two pieces of interfacing to fit them and iron on following the manufacturer's directions. With right sides together, pin and stitch along both long sides and one end. Snip the corners and turn the right way out and press.

6. Again using the paper pattern, cut out two pieces of plain fabric for the lining. With right sides together, if applicable, pin and stitch together along both sides. Slip over the patchwork bag, lining up the top raw edges of both. Push the strap piece between the patchwork bag and lining at the back, leaving the raw end slicking out slightly. Pin and machine stitch all the way round the top.

7. Turn the right way out. Fold the bottom of the lining bag in by ½in and machine stitch the bottom of the bag closed. Push the lining inside the bag.

8. Stitch one side of a snap to the under side of the strap and the other piece of the snap onto the bag. Sew a button onto the strap to finish.

Laundry Bag

Strips of fabric have been joined together to create this pretty, colorful laundry bag, perfect for storing clothes awaiting washing and stylish enough to hang in the bathroom. The flower is very simple to make and could be used to decorate many craft projects—or made up as a brooch, coordinating the fabrics with your outfit.

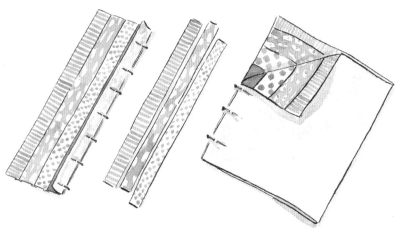

MATERIALS

4 x 43in piece of each of eight different fabrics
22 x 39in piece of fabric for the lining
22 x 39in piece of light-weight batting
Needle and thread
8 x 35in piece of iron-on interfacing
Button

3 hours

1. Measure and cut eight strips of fabric 2¾ x 41in. Lay them on the work surface until you are happy with the arrangement and then, with right sides together, pin and stitch the strips together. Press the seams open. Cut a strip vertically 4in wide from one side and put this aside to make the flower later.

2. Cut a piece of batting 18½ x 37in. Lay it onto the wrong side of the patchwork panel. Fold the batting and patchwork in half with the stripes running horizontally and match up the raw edges. Pin and stitch along the edge, and press the seam open.

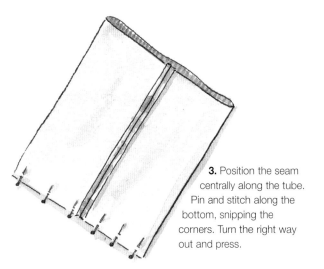

3. Position the seam centrally along the tube. Pin and stitch along the bottom, snipping the corners. Turn the right way out and press.

4. Measure and cut a piece of lining fabric 19½ x 37in. Fold in half and stitch along the side and bottom of it. Snip across the corners. Press ½in over to the wrong side around the top edge.

5. Slip the lining
inside the outer bag,
pushing it right into the corners
and ensuring that it lies flat. Fold the
pressed edge of the lining over the raw
edge of the outer bag and machine
stitch in place.

6. Measure and cut two pieces of fabric
2¾ x 32in. Iron interfacing to the back of both
pieces following the manufacturer's directions. With right
sides together, pin and stitch along both long sides and one
end. Snip the corners and turn the right way out. Turn the
end in by ⅛in and press. Hand stitch closed. Machine stitch
this strap onto the bag 4in from the right hand side on the
back and 4in from the left hand side on the front.

7. Take the strip from
step 1 and cut so that it
is seven panels of fabric
long. Cut a rounded
shape on each band of
fabric to form a petal
shape, either freehand or
draw a shape onto paper
and use as your pattern.

8. Make a running stitch along the
bottom of the strip and pull the
thread to gather it up to form the
flower. Finish with a few small
stitches and sew a button in the
center, sewing it onto the laundry
bag securely.

Lavender Pillow

Lavender bags have long been used to scent linens and help to provide a natural moth repellent. This lovely lavender bag is made from a simple cover decorated with scraps of pastel colored fabrics made into yo-yos. Yo-yos are so satisfying to make and create such a pretty way of decorating a plain project—they are finished here with an assortment of buttons. The cover has a muslin bag inside filled with dried lavender, which can easily be removed and replaced when the lavender loses its scent.

MATERIALS
8 x 20in piece of fabric for the pillow
Compass and pencil
Paper for pattern
6in square scraps of fabric for nine yo-yos
35½ x 1½in piece of fabric for the binding
35½in length of piping cord
Needle and thread
9 buttons
8 x 16in piece of muslin
Dried lavender

1½ hours

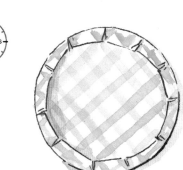

1. Using the compass, draw a circle 4¾in in diameter on the paper and cut out. Use this to cut out nine circles of fabric for the yo-yos. Using an iron, press about ¼in over to the wrong side all the way round each circle. Make a running stitch all the way round each fabric circle and pull the thread to gather the fabric into a yo-yo. Fasten the end of the thread securely with a few small stitches.

2. Measure and cut a 8⅜in square of fabric for the pillow. Cut a length of piping cord 35½in long and cover with a strip of fabric cut on the bias (see the techniques section on page 166), machine stitching it in place. Lay the piping all the way round the square of fabric matching the raw edges, Overlap the ends slightly, running the ends off the fabric. Pin and baste in place.

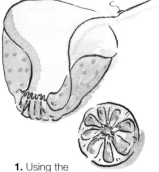

3. Measure and cut a rectangle of the pillow fabric 8⅜ x 6in and another piece 8⅜ x 4in. Press over ½in to the wrong side along one long edge on both pieces and fold this over again by ⅜in. Pin and machine stitch close to the first fold. Press. Lay the larger rectangle with right sides together onto the front of the pillow and position the second rectangle overlapping this, matching the raw edges. Pin and machine stitch all the way round the edge.

4. Snip the corners off and turn the right way out. Press. Hand stitch the yo-yos onto the front of the pillow with small stitches and finish with a button at the center of each. Stitch two squares of muslin 6¾in square together, leaving a small opening, and fill with dried lavender. Stitch the opening closed and put inside the pillow.

Coat Hanger

Padded coat hangers are much kinder to your clothes than wire ones and look prettier too. This project uses old embroidered napkins and linens that have seen better days, collected from flea markets and yard sales, and transforms them into a charming padded hanger that makes a feature of the delicate embroidery. Use a standard wooden hanger as the base, putting some dried lavender inside the cover before stitching it in place if you like, to add fragrance to your wardrobe.

1 hour

1. Using the template on page 169, make a paper pattern. With right sides together, join the strips of fabric so that the overall panel of fabrics is slightly bigger than the paper pattern. Pin the pattern onto the patchwork panel and cut out.

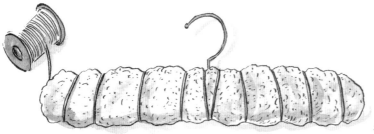

2. Pin the rickrack around the patchwork panel, overlapping the ends slightly. Machine stitch it in place, sewing along the center of the rickrack. Using the paper pattern, cut a piece for the back of the hanger from plain fabric.

3. Wrap a piece of batting around the coat hanger and hold in place with a length of thread, tying the ends to secure it.

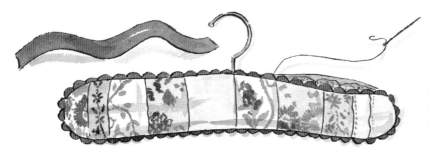

4. With right sides together, pin and stitch the front patchwork panel to the back piece, leaving an opening from one end to the middle along the top. Turn the cover the right way out. Press and slip over the padded hanger. Hand stitch the open edge of the cover closed. Tie a ribbon bow around the base of the hook to finish.

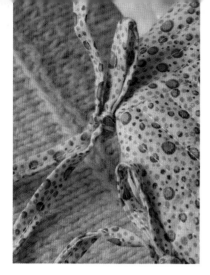

Hot Water Bottle Cover

Cozy up with this lovely hot water bottle cover, the perfect way to keep your toes toasty in the cold winter months. Made from panels of fine quilted fabric, it has an opening across the bottom making it easy to remove the hot water bottle for emptying and filling.

MATERIALS

20 x 24in piece of light-weight batting

10 x 14in pieces of three contrasting fabrics

20 x 14in piece of a fourth contrasting fabric

16 x 24in piece of lining fabric

3 self-cover buttons

Paper for patterns

3 hours

1. Using the templates on page 170, make paper patterns. Cut out two fabric pieces using pattern A. Cut out four of pattern B, using two different fabrics (so that you have two pieces of each fabric). Cut out two pieces using pattern C. With right sides together, pin and stitch a side panel to either side of the front center panel. Repeat to create a front and a back panel. Press the seams open.

2. With right sides together, pin and stitch piece C onto the main panel to form the neck. Press the seam toward the neck.

3. Lay the covers onto the batting and cut out the shape. Place the cover right side down onto the work surface and put the batting on top of it. Pin through both layers at the corners and the neck. Decide on the direction of the quilting and using the edge of the sewing foot on your machine as a guide, start to sew straight lines, working from the middle, out, sewing in different directions on each fabric section until the whole panel is quilted. Trim away the excess batting. Repeat for the second panel.

4. With right sides together, pin and stitch the two quilted panels together, leaving the bottom edge open. Snip the curved edges and the corners around the neck.

5. Double up the lining fabric by folding it in half. Place the quilted cover onto it and cut around the shape. Be generous so that the cover will not be too tight, and add ½in seam allowance all the way round. With right sides together, pin and stitch the two lining pieces together, leaving an opening at the top and bottom.

6. Cut eight strips of fabric 1 x 8in. Fold the fabric in half lengthwise and press. Fold the raw edges in toward the center and press. Machine stitch close to the edge.

7. With right sides together, place the hot water bottle cover inside the lining, ensuring that it fits snugly inside. Insert the ties through the open end between the layers of fabric, using four on each side. The main length of the ties should be concealed between the layers with just the ends sticking out slightly. Pin in place and machine stitch around the opening, stitching over the ties as you go. Pull the lining fabric over the hot water bottle cover through the opening in the neck. Slip stitch the neck end closed and push the lining into the cover.

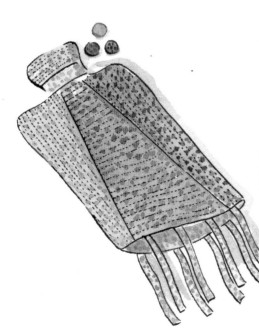

8. For the neck band, cut a strip on the bias about 1¼in wide and long enough to fit around the neck. Press under the raw edges along the length and hand stitch around the join of fabrics at the neck, folding under the end and stitching it in place neatly. Cover three buttons following the manufacturer's directions and sew them onto the neck. Put the hot water bottle inside the cover and tie the ties into neat bows.

2 hours

MATERIALS

12in square of fabric for base

4in piece of contrasting fabric

12in square of fabric for the sides

10in square of fabric for lining

12 x 22in square of light-weight batting

12in zipper

Cosmetics Bag

This stylish cosmetics bag is the perfect addition to your handbag and dressing table. Made with a border of small patchwork panels, it would make a much treasured and admired gift, too. The bag has been lined with a smart coordinating fabric but a waterproof lining could also be used to make it suitable for toiletries as well.

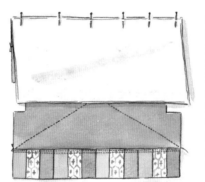

1. Cut out the base of the bag using the template on page 169. Find the center by folding it in half across the length and width, then mark from each corner with a diagonal line crossing the middle point. Fold and press along these lines. Cut a piece of batting slightly bigger than the base piece and pin around the edges and across the diagonal lines. Top stitch from corner to corner, creating a quilted diagonal cross. Cut away the excess batting.

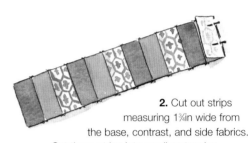

2. Cut out strips measuring 1¾in wide from the base, contrast, and side fabrics. Cut these strips into small rectangles measuring 1⅜ x 1¾in. Decide on the order of the rectangles and with right sides together, join all the rectangles together on their long edges to make two strips 9½in long. Press the seams open as you go.

3. Lay the base right side up on the work surface. Place one of the patchwork panels on top with right sides together. Pin and stitch together and press the seam toward the base. Join the other patchwork panel to the other side of the base and again press. Top stitch along the edge of the base on both sides.

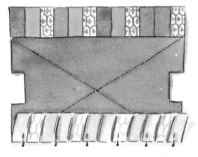

4. Cut two rectangles of fabric for the sides of the bag, each measuring 10 x 4½in. Cut two pieces of batting to fit them. Baste the batting to the wrong side of each side piece. With right sides together, pin and stitch the side pieces to the bottom panel. Press the seams towards the top and top stitch.

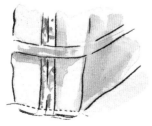

5. Fold the bag in half with right sides together and stitch down the sides. Trim away excess batting and press the seams open. Flatten the base and stitch across the bottom edges to close the corners. Trim.

6. Press in ½in along the top edge of the bag. With the zipper closed, baste it in place along one edge. Stitch into place ⅛in from the edge. Open the zipper and baste the other side of it to the other side of the bag. Stitch in place as before. Remove the basted stitches.

8. Press under ½in around the top edge and place inside the bag. Pin into position and hand stitch round the top just under the zipper.

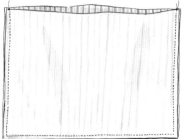

7. For the lining, cut out two rectangles 7¼in x 10in. Place with right sides together and join along one long edge and the two short sides. Press the seams open. Lay the sides across the length of the base and machine stitch across the corners. Cut off the excess.

Bordered Towel

Patchwork projects don't have to be complicated and time consuming. A store-bought towel can be embellished with an appealing border made from scraps of pretty fabrics in no time and this is another project that requires only small oddments of fabric. Make a set to give as a gift, stitching longer borders to sew onto bath towels, or coordinate a set with your own bathroom for a smart and stylish addition to your wash time.

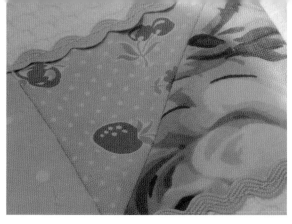

MATERIALS

4in square scraps of fabric in four shades of the same color

Purchased towel (the towel used here is 19¼in wide)

Rickrack braid twice the width of the towel plus 4in

Paper for template

1 hour

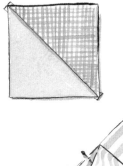

1. Using the template on page 173, make a paper pattern. Using the pattern, cut out two triangles from each shade of fabric so you have 16 fabric triangles (you will need more for a wider towel). Arrange them so that no two triangles of the same fabric are next to each other. With right sides together, pin and stitch two triangles together to form a square. Press the seam open. Continue with the remaining triangles, joining them to make eight squares in total.

2. Trim the seams to make neat squares. With right sides together, pin and stitch the squares together to form a strip. Press the seams open.

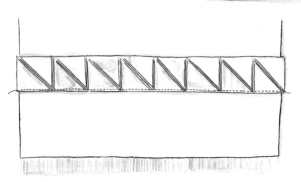

3. With right side down, lay the strip onto the towel 5in from the bottom. Pin it in place along the seam allowance. Stitch in place. Press ½in under along the other side and at each end.

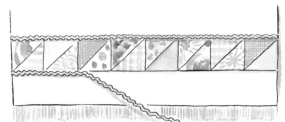

4. Fold the strip over on the towel so it is right side up, machine stitch the other edge in place, hand stitching the ends in place. Cut two lengths of rickrack 20½in long. Pin and stitch them along the top and bottom edge of the patchwork strip, folding the ends under neatly at the edge of the towel. Press.

CHAPTER 6

Outside Spaces

Green Purse

The large green spot fabric used in this bag is one of my favorites and I have used it in several sewing projects. I only had small scraps left, which was the inspiration for this bag—I mixed it with other green fabrics to create a cute purse. Edging the top of the bag with velvet ribbon adds a stylish trim, with a fabric rosette flower adding the finishing touch.

MATERIALS

Scraps of fabric in shades of green for the patchwork
20 x 16in fabric for the side gussets, back and base
24 x 16in plain fabric for the lining
32 x 18½in cotton batting
16 x 6in plain fabric
14 x 5½in patterned fabric
32in length of velvet ribbon
Button

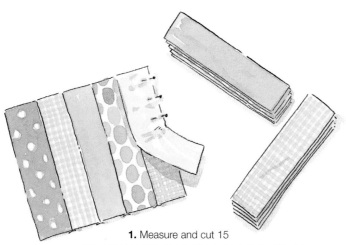

1. Measure and cut 15 strips of assorted pieces of green fabric 2 x 8in. Lay them out side by side and move them around until you are happy with the arrangement. With right sides together, pin and stitch them together with a ½in seam, pressing the seams open as you go until all the strips are joined together.

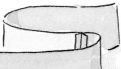

2. Measure and cut a strip of fabric 16 x 2½in for the base. Cut two strips 8 x 2½in for the side gussets. With right sides together, pin and stitch each short piece to either end of the longer piece. Press all the seams open.

3. Measure and cut a piece of batting 16 x 8in and lay the patchwork panel right side up on to it. Cut a strip of batting 32 x 2½in. Lay this onto the wrong side of the gusset and base strip. Place this with right sides together onto the patchwork panel, lining up the raw edges along one long side. Pin in place.

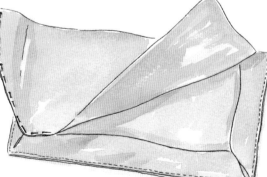

4. Lay the side gussets along the edges of the patchwork panel, with the batting in place and pin and stitch in place. Make a snip at both corners in the seam allowance. Cut a rectangle of fabric and a panel of batting both measuring 16 x 8in. With right sides together and with the batting on the wrong side, pin and stitch the back of the bag onto the side gussets and base of the bag, again snipping the corners of the seam allowance.

5. Cut two rectangles of lining fabric measuring 16 x 8in and a side and base strip of lining fabric measuring 32 x 2½in. Stitch the long strip along both ends and one long side of one of the rectangles. Snip the corners. Stitch the remaining rectangle to the other side of the side and base strip to form the lining. Press.

6. With wrong sides together, push the lining inside the bag, lining up the base and corners. Pin a length of ribbon around the top of the outside of the bag and machine stitch in place about ⅝in from the edge. Overlap the ends of the ribbon neatly. Fold the ribbon over to the inside of the bag and hand stitch all the way round.

7. Cut two strips of plain fabric measuring 13 x 2in and two strips of patterned fabric the same size. With right sides together, pin and stitch one plain strip to one patterned strip along one end and both long sides. Turn the strip the right way out and fold in the remaining raw end by ½in. Hand stitch closed. Repeat with the other two strips to form the second handle. Hand stitch both the handles securely onto the bag on the inside.

8. To make the flower, cut a strip of plain fabric measuring 2 x 16in and a strip of patterned fabric 1½ x 14in. Make a running stitch along one long side of each of the strips and gather to form two rosette shapes. Hand stitch them together with a button in the middle and sew the flower onto the bag securely.

Striped Tote Bag

The sophisticated look of this bag belies its simplicity. Made from wide panels of fabric joined to make the outer bag, it has a yoke across the top of the front and the back with a gathered lining. It all makes for a roomy bag suitable for both day and evening use.

MATERIALS

26 x 30in piece of blue spotted fabric for stripe and lining

26 x 16in piece of gray spotted fabric for stripe and handles

26 x 30in piece of cream fabric for stripe and side gussets

Iron-on interfacing

Paper for pattern

2 hours

1. Measure and cut out six 3½ x 23½in strips of three different fabrics. With right sides together, pin and stitch two of the strips together, and press the seam open.

2. Continue to join the strips together to form a panel. Measure and cut a piece of interfacing the same size as the panel. Following the manufacturer's directions, iron this onto the wrong side of the panel.

3. Measure and cut two 4¾ x 10in rectangles of the cream fabric for the side gussets. Iron interfacing onto the wrong side of both pieces. With right sides together, pin and stitch the gussets onto the main panel, starting and finishing the stitching ½in from the top edge. Snip off the corner seam allowances.

4. To make the handles measure and cut four 1¾ x 16in rectangles of gray spotted fabric. Iron interfacing to the wrong side of all of them. With right sides together, pin and stitch along both long sides and turn the right way out. Press.

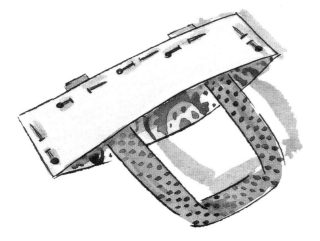

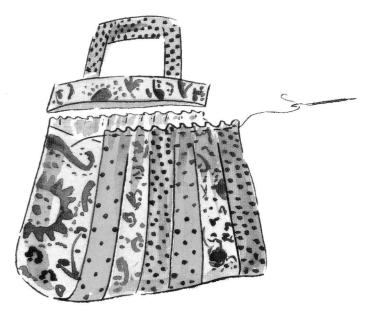

5. To make the band across the top of the bag, measure and cut four 3 x 12⅛in rectangles. Again iron interfacing to the back of them. With right sides together, pin around three sides to join two of them together. Insert the ends of one of the handles between the two layers so that the ends stick out slightly through the seam. Stitch in place. Repeat with the other two pieces and the other handle.

6. Make a running stitch along each side of the patchwork bag and gather it up so that it will fit exactly inside the top band. With right sides together, pin and stitch the gathered edge of the bag to the outer side of the top bar on both sides of the bag.

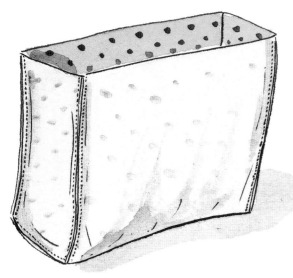

7. Measure and cut one 23 x 16in rectangle of lining fabric and two 4¾ x 10in rectangles. In the same way as the outer bag, with right sides together, pin and stitch the side gussets to the main fabric, again starting and finishing the stitching ½in from the top edge to form a bag. Press the seams open and snip the corners.

8. Slip the lining bag over the outer bag with right sides together. Pin and stitch across the top of the gussets. Turn the lining the right way out and push into the bag. Make a running stitch across the top of both sides of the lining fabric so that it is the same width as the outer bag. Turn under ½in to the wrong side on the top bands and pin and hand stitch in place along the lining. Press.

Picnic Blanket

This lovely vintage-style picnic blanket is made from an old floral tablecloth that was stained in places and could no longer be used. Squares of this have been joined with plain pink fabric to make the main panel, which has been edged with gingham and trimmed with a contrasting ribbon and buttons. Use heavy-weight batting and a cotton fabric backing to make a hardy blanket that will make your picnic as comfortable and enjoyable as can be.

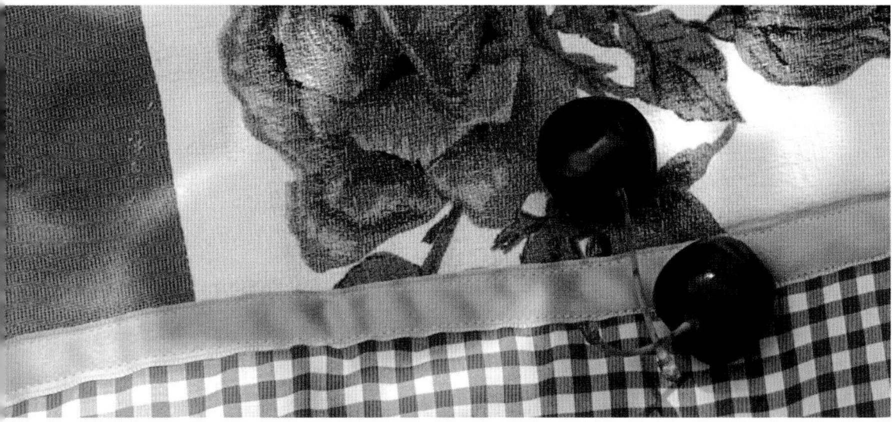

2 hours

MATERIALS

40 x 20in of plain fabric
36 x 20in of floral fabric
36 x 20in piece of gingham fabric
41in square of spotted fabric for the backing
40in square of cotton batting
148in length of ribbon
4 buttons

1. Cut a paper square measuring 8½in. Use this to cut out eight squares of plain fabric and eight squares of floral fabric. Lay them alternately in a block of four squares by four. With right sides together, pin and stitch the squares together in strips with a ¼in seam to form four strips. Press the seams open.

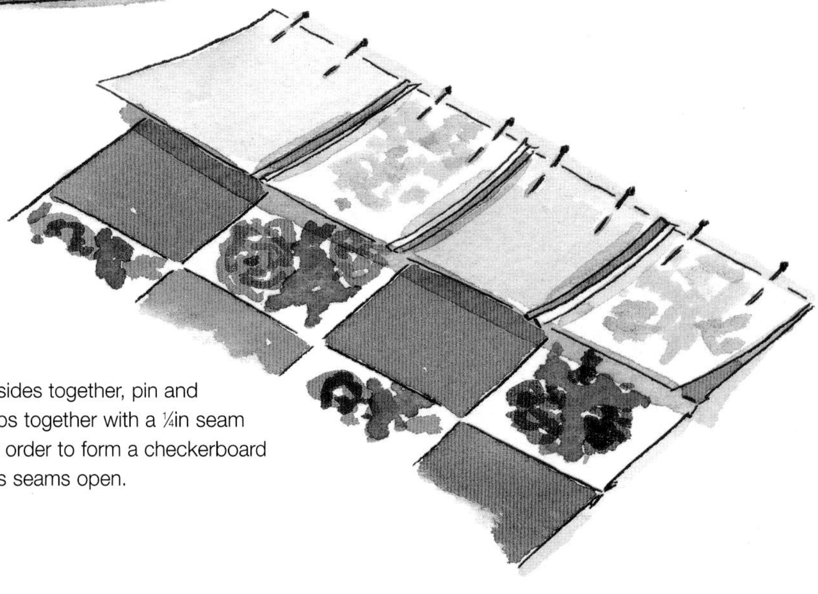

2. With right sides together, pin and stitch the strips together with a ¼in seam in the correct order to form a checkerboard pattern. Press seams open.

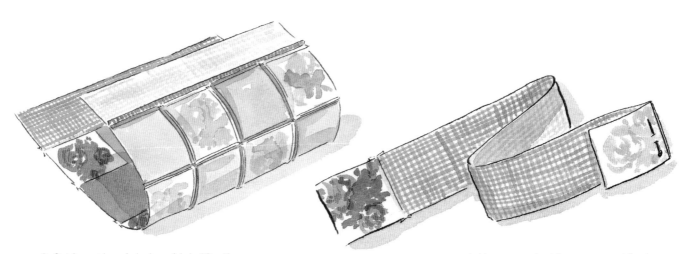

3. Cut four strips of gingham fabric 33 x 5in. Take one of the strips and with right sides together, pin, and stitch it with a ½in seam along one side of the patchwork panel. Stitch another length and stitch it to the opposite side of the patchwork panel. Press the seams open.

4. Measure and cut four squares of floral fabric 5in. With right sides together, pin and stitch one floral square onto each end of the two remaining gingham strips with a ½in seam and press the seams open.

5. With right sides together, pin and stitch the gingham strips with the floral fabric squares onto the patchwork panel, with a ½in seam. Press the seams open.

6. Measure and cut a piece of spotted fabric for the backing 41in square. With right sides together, pin and stitch this to the patchwork panel with a ½in seam, leaving an opening of about 14in. Trim the corners and turn the right way out. Press.

7. Cut a piece of batting 40in square. Push this into the cover making sure that the corners of the batting sit snugly into the corners of the cover. Ensure that the batting lies completely flat. Pin all the layers together. Hand stitch the opening closed.

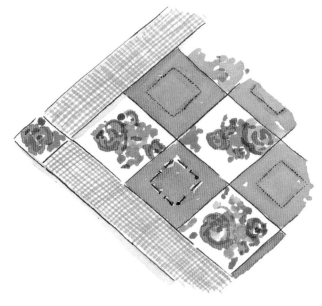

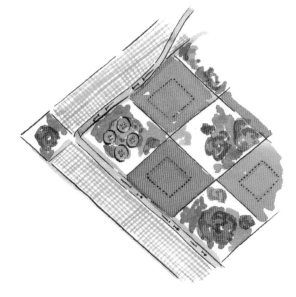

8. Marking the position with pins (or masking tape if you find that easier), measure a square on each of the plain patchwork squares and machine stitch through all layers.

9. Pin and stitch ribbon along the edge of the border to cover the join, folding the ribbon neatly at the corners and stitching along both edges of it. Finish with a button sewn onto each corner of the ribbon.

Beach Bag

This beach bag is most definitely as practical as it is good looking. Made from hard-wearing natural linen, it has handy pockets for sunglasses, phone, and other essentials on one side, a large pocket on the other side, ideal for holding a Frisbee, and enough room inside to hold everything you will need for a fun day at the seaside. Metal eyelets are available from notions stores and give a smart professional finish when combined with thick rope used as handles, perfectly in keeping with the seaside theme.

MATERIALS

20 x 42in piece of upholstery-weight linen
20 x 32in piece of fabric for lining
14 x 20in pieces of four different fabrics for pockets
4 eyelets
Eyelet machine
48in length of rope for handles

4 hours

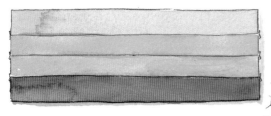

1. To make the pockets, cut a strip from each of the four coordinating fabrics measuring 32 x 2½in. With right sides together, pin and stitch the strips together along the long edges and press the seams open. Cut a piece 12½in long by the depth of the strip for the Frisbee pocket. Cut a piece 7in long for the flat pocket and a piece 10½in long for the folded pocket. To create the seam covers, cut strips of three of the fabrics 1in wide by the widths of the two smaller pockets. Fold the raw edges in toward the center by ¼in and press. Place these strips over the seams of the pocket fronts and top stitch them in place.

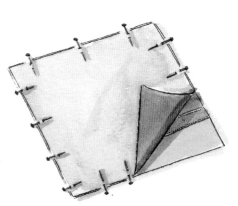

2. Lay the pocket fronts onto the lining fabric and cut out a piece of lining for each. Place each pocket front right sides together with its lining piece and stitch all the way round, leaving a small opening. Snip off the corners and turn the pocket right way out. Press. Repeat for all three pockets.

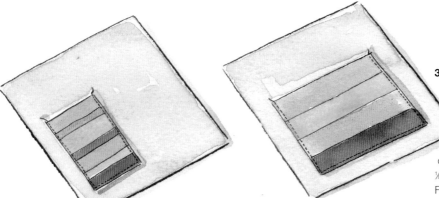

3. Cut out two pieces of linen each 19¼in square. Lay these onto the work surface right sides up. Place the flat pocket about 5¼in from the top and pin and stitch in place around three sides, leaving an opening at the top and stitching about ⅛in from the edge. Repeat this with the Frisbee pocket on the second linen square.

4. Take the folded pocket piece and mark the center with pins. Make a fold approximately ⅝in deep, bring it toward the center mark, and pin in place at the base. Repeat at the other side. Using a scrap of fabric, cut a strip 3 x 1in. Press in half lengthwise, open out, and press in raw edges to the center fold. Machine stitch close to the edge. Make it into a loop and hand stitch it onto one side of the pocket pleat. Position this pocket onto the bag front and stitch in place along three sides. Sew a button onto the other side of the pocket so you can fit the loop over it.

5. With the linen pieces right sides together, pin and stitch along both sides and the bottom of the bag. Press the seams open. Sew across the corners diagonally to form a base. Turn top over to the wrong side by 3in to create a yoke and press along the folded edge. Turn the bag right side out and open out the yoke again.

6. Cut two rectangles of fabric 19¼ x 15¾in for the lining. With right sides together, pin and stitch along the two shorter sides and across the bottom, then press the seams open. As with the main bag pieces, sew diagonally across the corners to create a base.

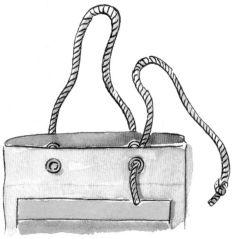

7. To join the lining to the bag, slip the lining over the linen bag with right sides together. Match the side seams and pin in place. At the top edge, align the raw edges of the yoke on the main fabric and the lining, and machine stitch around them leaving an opening of about 5in. Remove the pins at the sides and then turn the lining right side out through the opening and push it into the bag. Hand stitch the opening closed.

8. Mark the position for the eyelets on the front and the back of the bag, about 6in in from each outer edge. Following the manufacturer's directions, fix the eyelets in place. Thread a length of rope around 24in long through two eyelets and tie the ends into knots. Repeat through the other two eyelets.

Bunting

When making sewing projects, there are inevitably lots of leftover pieces of fabric. Bunting is a quick and easy way of using up these scraps to create a cute decoration for just about anywhere in the home. Mix colors and patterns using different fabrics on each side of each triangle, finishing the bunting with simple flower and button embellishments and stitching them onto ribbon.

1 hour

MATERIALS

Scraps of fabrics at least 10 x 11in

Paper for pattern

Buttons

Ribbon

1. Using the template on page 168, cut out a paper pattern. Decide how many bunting triangles you would like and cut two fabric triangles for each one. With right sides together, pin and stitch two fabric triangles together, starting and finishing the stitches ⅞in from the top edge.

2. Trim the seam allowance and turn the triangles the right way out. Press. Turn in ½in to the wrong side along both top edges of each triangle.

3. Slip the ribbon between the top opening of the triangles, and pin and stitch in place with a double row of stitches.

4. Using the templates on page 168, cut out a large and a small flower shape from paper and use them to cut out a large and small fabric flower for each triangle. Hand stitch the flowers onto the triangles, sewing a button in the middle of each.

Purse

A very simple patchwork project has been enhanced with simple embroidery stitches (see the techniques section for these stitches) to make this sweet purse with a store-bought (or homemade if you crochet as well as sew!) flower to decorate it. The purse has been lined with pretty fabric and could easily be made on a larger scale and used as a clutch bag—or a shoulder bag if a strap is attached.

3 hours

1. Measure and cut four strips of linen 2¼ x 12in. With right sides together, pin and stitch them together. Press the seams open.

2. Following the instructions on the techniques pages, embroider a fly stitch along the outer joins of the patchwork strips, a cross-stitch along another one, and a zigzag stitch along the remaining one.

3. Measure and cut a rectangle 8 x 12in from the lining fabric. With right sides together, pin and stitch the patchwork panel to the lining fabric, leaving an opening of about 2in along one side. Snip the corners off and turn the right way out. Press and hand stitch the opening closed.

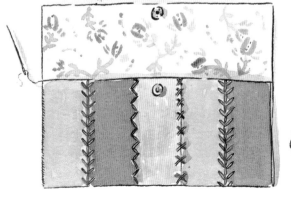

4. Fold the fabric over by 4in and stitch down both sides. Stitch one side of the snap to the middle of the purse, near the top edge, and the other half to the underside of the flap. Stitch a flower onto the purse to decorate it.

Techniques

Basic equipment

Most of the equipment that is needed for quilting will probably already be part of your sewing kit. Specific tools are listed under the Materials list for each project but here are the "basics" that you will need throughout this book:

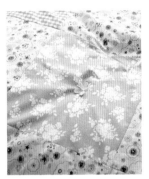

Sewing machine
A sewing machine is essential, although a basic model is all that is required. It is advisable to replace the needles regularly, especially when quilting, to keep them nice and sharp. Special quilting needles are available and are good for stitching through thick layers.

Scissors
You will need a pair of large shears for cutting fabrics—which need to be kept really sharp—a pair of small embroidery scissors for cutting seam allowances and snipping threads, and a pair of good craft scissors for cutting patterns.

Rotary cutter and mat
This tool allows you to cut through several layers very accurately and saves a lot of time if you have lots of patchwork pieces to cut. The blade needs to be kept very sharp and must be handled with care. A self-healing mat provides an ideal surface for cutting. Rotary rulers are available but a standard acrylic ruler will be fine. A square can also be useful.

Rotary cutter

Pins
Long, sharp pins will be needed and safety pins can be useful for keeping layers of quilting together while working on them. Special quilter's pins are available that have a flat head, which can be useful for machine quilting.

Iron
This is essential for quilting and is used throughout all the projects here. Pressing seams open creates a neat professional finish and makes sewing patchwork much easier.

Dressmaker's chalk pencil
This is needed for making temporary marks on fabric to mark stitching lines and can be brushed off easily.

Pattern paper
This paper is marked with equally spaced horizontal and vertical lines and is used to make pattern pieces.

Fabrics

Fabrics should be prewashed and ironed when making patchwork and quilting. When piecing small patches of fabric together it can be useful to spray a little starch onto the fabric to make it slightly stiffer. Generally, it is a good idea to use fabrics of a similar weight in a project, with cotton and linen fabrics being the easiest to handle. The colors used are important as lighter and darker tones can change the look and focus of patchwork and different colors and patterns can create very different effects. Plain fabrics and stripes are useful for backing quilts.

Batting

There is a selection of this available from fabric and quilting stores in a variety of widths and thickness. Cotton batting is the most expensive and is often not washable (consult the manufacturer's directions) but it drapes beautifully and gives a lovely soft finish. Polyester batting is the cheaper option, is machine washable, and gives a slightly stiffer finish. As with fabrics, it is advisable to wash the batting before using it.

Templates

To make a template for a fabric shape, enlarge or reduce it on a photocopier to the required size. If you are cutting out with scissors, simply cut out the photocopied shape and pin it to the fabric to use as a pattern piece. If you are using a rotary cutter to cut your fabric you will need to make a card template. Trace the motif onto tracing paper. Turn the tracing paper over and scribble over the drawn lines with a pencil. Turn the tracing paper over again and place on a piece of card. Draw over the lines and the shape will be transferred to the card. Cut the shape out and use as your pattern piece.

Piecing

This means joining pieces of fabric together to form larger panels. I have generally used a seam allowance of ⅛in throughout this book, which means that you stitch exactly ⅛in from the raw edge. Use the stitching guide on your sewing machine if there is one, or measure from the machine needle and stick a piece of masking tape onto the stitching plate to use as your guide.

When piecing lots of shapes (for a quilt, say) stitch them in a chain and then cut the threads, which speeds things up and saves thread too.

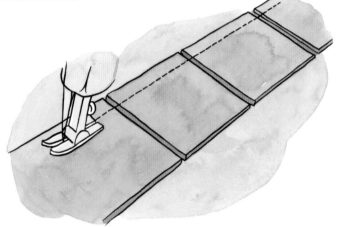

Chain piecing

Quilting

There are several ways to hold the layers of patchwork together to quilt them. Machine quilting is a quick and easy way to do this and is effective on large quilted projects. To stitch straight lines, masking tape can be stuck onto the surface of the fabric to act as a guide for the stitching, or dressmaker's chalk can be used. Ditch quilting is when the quilt is stitched along the seams of patchwork, making the stitches virtually invisible. Contour quilting is when the quilt is stitched within the patchwork, creating a slightly raised effect.

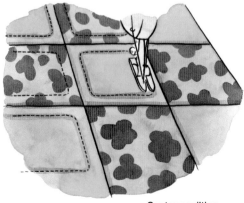

Contour quilting

Hand quilting gives a lovely finish to a quilted project but is time consuming and not suitable for large projects if you are after quick results. A running stitch can be made through all the layers in straight lines or a more random pattern.

Tied quilting is a quick way of quilting a large area. Stitch embroidery thread through the quilt from the right side to the wrong side leaving a long end. Stitch back up to the wrong side about ⅛in away from the first stitch and then make a few more stitches in this way ending with the thread on the right side. Tie the ends with a neat knot and trim.

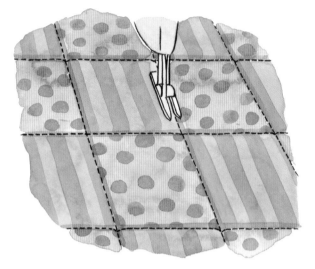

Ditch quilting

Tied quilting

Buttons

Buttons are an effective way of quilting layers. Stitch the buttons onto the fabric through all the layers to hold them in place.

Binding

Binding is used to edge several projects in this book. To bind straight edges, strips of fabric cut on the straight of grain can be used. To bind curves or make piping cord, you will need to cut fabric strips on the bias:

1 Using a square and chalk, mark lines about 1½in apart at a 45° angle across the fabric and cut along them.

2 To join strips together, pin and stitch the ends together along the straight edge. Press the seam open and trim the ends of the seams.

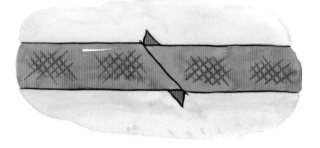

3 Continue to join the strips together until the bias strip is the required size for your project.

Piping cord

Piping cord finishes sewing projects off beautifully, adding a tailored, neat finish.

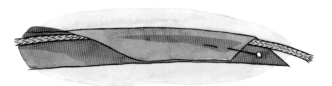

1 Cut a strip of cord (available in a range of thicknesses) to the desired length. Make a bias strip long enough to cover it. Fold the fabric strip in half lengthwise with wrong sides together and push the cord inside. Pin along the fabric, pushing the cord into the central fold.

2 Using the zipper foot on your machine, stitch along the fabric as close to the cord as you can get.

Stitches

Basting stitch is used to temporarily hold pieces of fabric together until they have been sewn permanently, when the basting can be removed. Use a contrasting color of thread to make the stitches easy to see.

Running stitch is a very simple stitch to do and is used to gather a strip of fabric. Bring the needle up to the right side and push it down again, bringing it back up again in a straight line. Continue as required.

Slip stitch is used in lots of the projects in this book. It is used to close openings and to secure hems and bindings in place. Make small evenly spaced stitches through the fold or layers of fabric to be joined, and finish with a few small stitches at the end to hold it in place, working from right to left.

Embroidery stitches can add the finishing touch to a project.

Fly stitch—take a horizontal stitch, bringing the needle up in the middle, a little bit lower down over the thread, then make a vertical stitch.

Cross-stitch—bring the needle up to the right side and make a small diagonal stitch. Bring the needle up to the right side again in line with the first stitch and make another diagonal stitch across the first.

Zigzag stitch—bring the needle up through to the right side and make a diagonal stitch. Bring the needle up to the right side again and make a diagonal stitch in the opposite direction, joining it to the end of the first stitch.

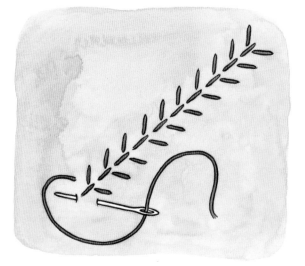

Fly stitch

Templates

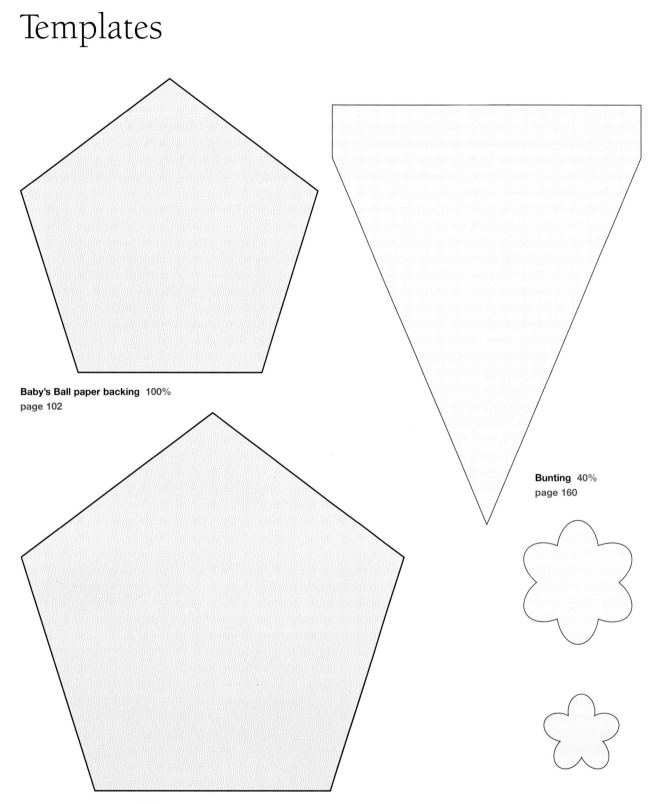

Baby's Ball paper backing 100%
page 102

Bunting 40%
page 160

Baby's Ball fabric piece 100%
page 102

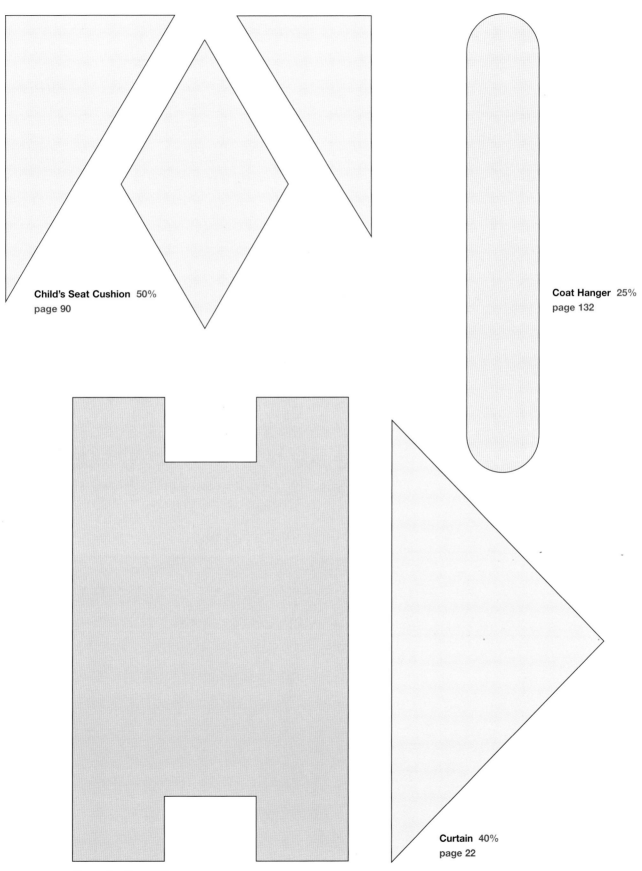

Child's Seat Cushion 50%
page 90

Coat Hanger 25%
page 132

Cosmetics Bag 50%
page 138

Curtain 40%
page 22

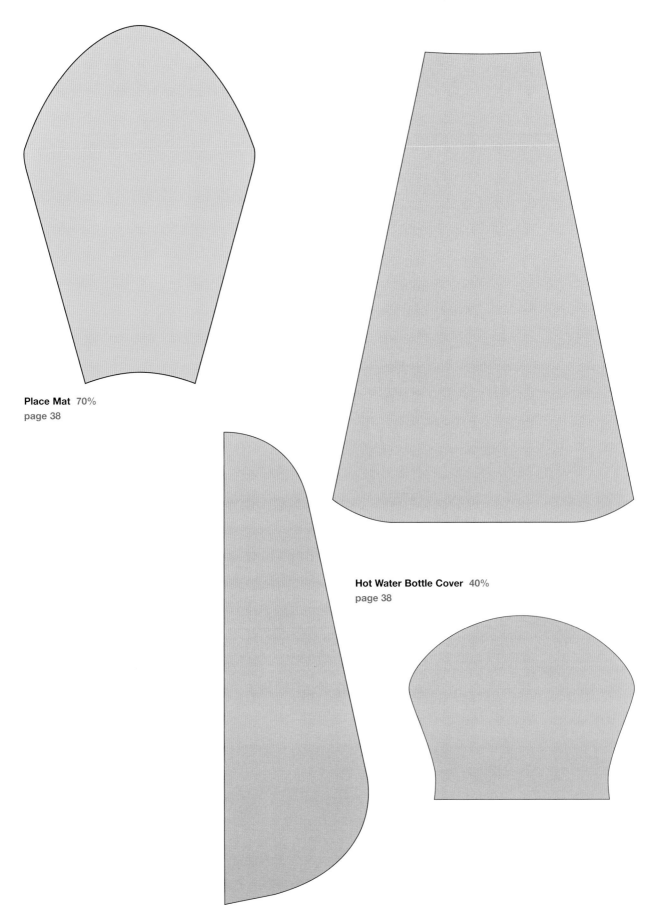

Place Mat 70%
page 38

Hot Water Bottle Cover 40%
page 38

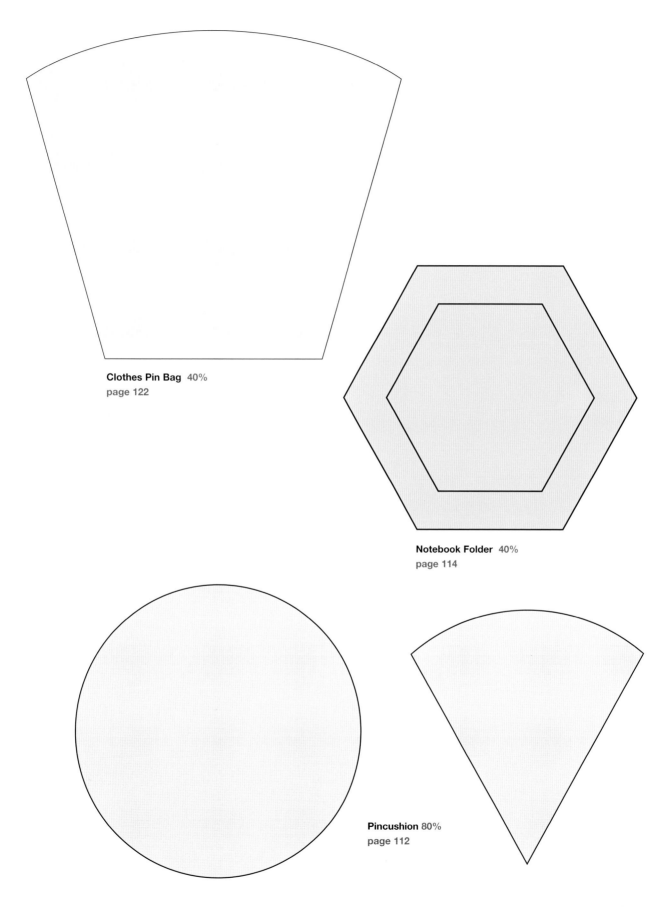

Clothes Pin Bag 40%
page 122

Notebook Folder 40%
page 114

Pincushion 80%
page 112

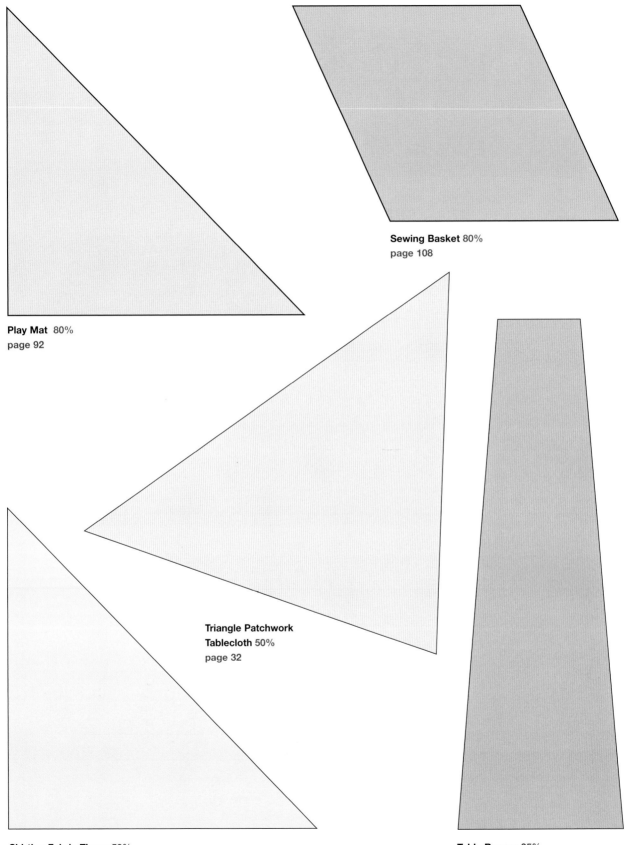

Sewing Basket 80%
page 108

Play Mat 80%
page 92

**Triangle Patchwork
Tablecloth** 50%
page 32

Shirting Fabric Throw 50%
page 62

Table Runner 35%
page 40

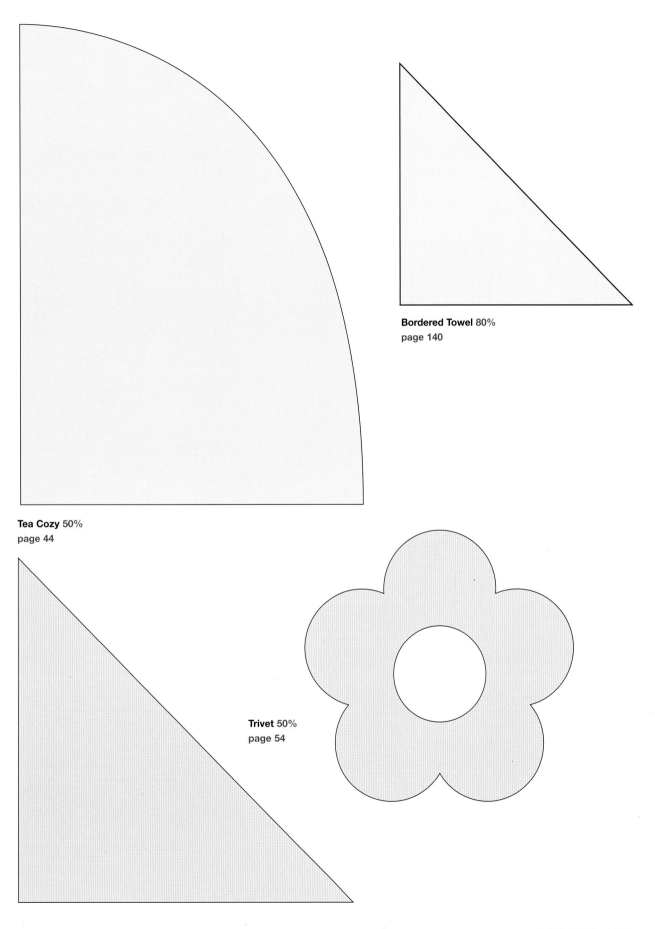

Bordered Towel 80%
page 140

Tea Cozy 50%
page 44

Trivet 50%
page 54

Suppliers

UK STOCKISTS

The Button Queen
19 Marylebone Lane
London W1V 2NF
020 7935 1505
www.thebuttonqueen.co.uk

Cath Kidston
08450 262 440
www.cathkidston.co.uk

The Cloth House
47 Berwick Street
London W1F 8SJ
020 7437 5155
www.clothhouse.com

Fabrics Galore
52–54 Lavender Hill
London SW11 5RH
020 7738 9589

Ian Mankin
109 Regent's Park Road
London NW1 8UR
020 7722 0997
www.ianmankin.com

Laura Ashley
0871 230 2301
www.lauraashley.com

John Lewis
Oxford Street
London W1A 1EX
020 7629 7711
www.johnlewis.com

Liberty
Regent Street
London W1B 5AH
020 7734 1234
www.liberty.co.uk

The Little Fabric Shop
www.littlefabric.com

The Quilt Room
20 West Street
Dorking
Surrey RH4 1BL
01306 740439
www.quiltroom.co.uk

Tikki Patchwork
293 Sandycombe Road
Kew
Surrey TW9 3LU
020 8948 8462
www.tikkilondon.com

VV Rouleaux
102 Marylebone Lane
London W1U 2QD
020 7224 5179
www.vvrouleaux.com

US STOCKISTS

Amy Butler
www.amybutler.com

Britex Fabrics
146 Geary Street
San Francisco
CA 94108
415-392-2910
www.britexfabrics.com

Cia's Palette
4155 Grand Ave S
Minneapolis
MN 55409
612-229-5227
www.ciaspalette.com

Purl Patchwork
147 Sullivan Street
New York
NY 10012
212-420-8798
www.purlsoho.com

Reprodepot Fabrics
413-527-4047
www.reprodepot.com

Tinsel Trading Company
47 West 38th Street
New York
NY 10018
212-730-1030
www.tinseltrading.com

Z and S Fabrics
681 S. Muddy Creek Road
Denver
PA 17157
717-336-4026
www.zandsfabrics.com

Index

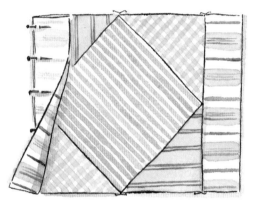

Acknowledgments

A big thank you to Debbie Patterson for the beautiful photography as ever, and for boundless enthusiasm and good humor throughout the project.

Thank you Michael Hill for the beautiful illustrations and being such a pleasure to work with. Thank you to Marie Clayton for editing the book with such attention to detail and to Pete Jorgensen and Sally Powell at CICO for all your unstinting help and support. Many thanks to Cindy Richards for trusting me to do this book in the first place.

A big thank you to Beverlee Regan, for designing and making the beach bag, hot water bottle cover, and cosmetics bag so beautifully. Thank you to Sandesh Brown, for your very good taste in wool. A huge thank you to Gracie and Betty for all your enthusiasm and encouragement and for many, many helpful suggestions and ideas. And of course, thank you to Laurie Dahl for endless amounts of patience and constant reassurances that I would meet my deadlines. You were right, although it was a close call at times!